c

THE TRAITS OF
WOMEN OF
GRACE

CRYSTAL D. HARRISON, M. ED
FOREWORD BY: BISHOP KIM A. DAVIS

CO-AUTHOR APPEARANCES BY

LETRICIA BROWN
ELIZABETH BUTLER
SABRINA CLEMONS
KATYCE JONES
MARGARET MARIE WARE

CARLA SMITH
CAROL BRYANT
MARY COLLINS
HELEN BOWMAN
BRENDA ABREU-BAKER

The Traits of Women of Grace
Copyright © 2023 by Crystal D. Harrison, Elizabeth Butler, Carla Smith, Sabrina Clemons, Helen Bowman, Mary Collins, Katyce Jones, Letricia Brown, Carol Bryant, Margaret Marie Ware, Brenda Abreu-Baker, Kim A. Davis.

Published by Grace 4 Purpose, Publishing Co. LLC

.

Scriptures taken from the Holy Bible, New International Version®, NIV®. Copyright © 1973, 1978, 1984, 2011 by Biblica, Inc.™ Used by permission of Zondervan. All rights reserved worldwide. www.zondervan.com The "NIV" and "New International Version" are trademarks registered in the United States Patent and Trademark Office by Biblica, Inc.™

Scripture quotations from The Authorized (King James) Version. Rights in the Authorized Version in the United Kingdom are vested in the Crown. Reproduced by permission of the Crown's patentee, Cambridge University Press.

Scripture quotations are taken from Good News Translation® (Today's English Version, Second Edition). Copyright © 1992 American Bible Society. All rights reserved.

ISBN- 979-8-9879298-2-7
Book cover design by Untouchable Designz and Consulting
Printed and bound in the United States of America

TABLE OF CONTENTS

DEDICATION

This book is written by women for women regardless of what or where you have traveled in this journey called life. These pages contain the testimonials of eleven women who have allowed their lives to be used in this Co-Author project to impact the lives of you, the reader, forevermore.

Proverbs 27:17 "As iron sharpens iron, so one person sharpens another." Who sharpens you is critical in being able to reach your fullest potential.

Each WOG with a unique assignment on their lives from the Father to impact lives one opportunity at a time. I pray that after reading "Women of Grace," you will allow your life to be used as a living testimony that will impact the hearts of women everywhere.

FOREWORD

For centuries, women have been the backbone of society. They have stood strong in adverse situations while being discounted on the world stage. Women have been the nurturers of mankind while placing their own hopes and dreams on the back burner or removing them from the table all together. Yet, they have continued to show up faithfully carrying out their assignment whatever that may be.

In recent times, women have forged their way to the forefront and are leading in unprecedented areas. They are not only leading but flourishing with poise, confidence and strength. What is it that empowers women to stand and persevere for centuries? It is the grace of God! The Holy Spirit described that grace to me as being "the supernatural ability of God to do for you what you can't do for yourself." Because of that grace women have stood strong on shaky ground, traveled roads with no real direction, and remained when everything had fallen apart.

This book is written by one of those women who have experienced so many aspects of life that broke her, yet she stands strong because of the grace of God on her life. And today she brings together other women who possess these same distinguishing qualities. The book is designed to inspire and fortify women of all walks of life. It will help them to recognize the coat of many colors the Father has placed upon each of us. As you read I know you won't be disappointed.

Sincerely,

Bishop Kim A. Davis

Alliance of Eagles Fellowship, Inc.

Presiding, Prelate

Chapter One Elizabeth Butler

A Life of Prayer

Early in Jesus' public ministry you will discover the necessity of prayer. Prayer is simply our communication with God, our Heavenly Father. As women of God, or simply as believers in the Lord, we have access to God through prayer. *"Now in the morning, having risen a long while before daylight, He went out and departed to a solitary place; and there He prayed" (Mark 1:35 NKJV)*. Jesus went to a solitary place to talk to God. A solitary place is an isolated place; sometimes it can be a lonely place, but most of all it's a necessary place. It's when you, as a woman of God, can openly communicate with our heavenly Father. It is a time of intimacy with the King of Kings and the Lord of Lords, where you can express your inner thoughts, feelings, emotions, and fears about this journey called life.

It's in the secret place with the Most High God where you know your supplications and petitions are heard. *"Now this is the confidence that we have in Him, that if we ask anything according to His will, He hears us" (1 John 5:14 NKJV)*. Therefore, when you pray, know that God is listening. A life of prayer is essential for the believer because it gives God the legal right and permission to intervene in your earthly affairs. *"If My people who are called by My name will humble themselves, and pray and seek My face, and turn from their wicked ways, then I will hear from heaven, and will forgive their sin and heal their land" (2 Chronicles 7:14 NKJV)*. The power of prayer is not the result of the person praying, but rather the power resides in the God who is being prayed to. *"God has spoken once, twice I have heard this; that power belongs to God" (Psalms 62:11 NKJV)*.

THE AUTHORITY OF PRAYER

There are different types of prayers that can be prayed while in the secret place with our heavenly Father. *"Praying always with all prayer and supplication in the spirit" (Ephesians 6:18 NKJV).* The Bible tells us that we should always pray with all kinds of prayers. Even though prayers can be different, they are equally powerful. Each and every day of our lives should include prayer due to the different challenges or obstacles that we may face at one time or another. Jesus said, *"And whatever you ask in My name, that I will do, that the Father may be glorified in the Son. If you ask anything in My name, I will do it" (John 14:13-14 NKJV).* The authority of prayer resides with all power in the name of Jesus. This is why Jesus could boldly declare that, *"All authority has been given to Me in heaven and on earth" (Matthew 28:18 NKJV).* Therefore, as a woman of God, you have full authority and power to pray in the name of Jesus Christ, the son of the living God. As a result, when you pray, know that something has to shift and move in the spirit realm on your behalf. The Bible declares, *"Assuredly, I say to you, whatever you bind on earth will be bound in heaven, and whatever you loose on earth will be loosed in heaven" (Mathew 18:18 NKJV).*

According to the book of Genesis Chapter 1, we understand that God created us in His image and after His likeness. He then commanded us to be fruitful, to multiply, fill the earth, subdue it, and most of all have dominion. To have dominion means through the person of the Holy Spirit, we possess the power to rule, the right to govern, and to exercise authority. Jesus gave this authority to his own disciples. *"Then He called His twelve disciples together and gave them power and authority over all demons, and to cure diseases. He sent them to preach the kingdom of God and to heal the sick" (Luke 9:1-2 NKJV).* Jesus expected them to exercise spiritual authority by putting into action what they had learned from Him; which included fervent prayer and unshakeable faith. The Bible says that the effective, fervent prayer of a righteous man avails much (James 5:16 NKJV). When we have faith and pray with authority, we should see the Word of God work on our behalf. You will decree a thing and it shall be established (Job 22:28 NKJV).

THE PRAYER OF THANKSGIVING

We should always begin our prayers with a heart of thanksgiving unto the Lord. *"Enter into His gates with thanksgiving, and into His courts with praise. Be thankful to Him, and bless His name" (Psalms 100:4 NKJV).* A simple thank you or showing the Lord gratitude, is imperative when we enter into prayer. God has done so much for His children and continues to do things for us each and every day that sometimes we merely forget to just say thank you. *"For God so loved the world that He gave His only begotten son, that whoever believes in Him should not perish but have eternal life" (John 3:16 NKJV).* The fact alone that God gave His only son's life so that we can live eternally with Him if we believe is more than reason enough to thank Him.

We should also thank the Lord for providing His divine protection for us, for His grace and mercies renewed daily for us, for allowing us to wake up each and every day of our lives, for good health, for prospering us, etc. The list goes on and on. However, the purpose of thanking the Lord is to show Him our appreciation for Him and what He continues to do for His children. *"Oh that men would give thanks to the Lord for His goodness, and for His wonderful works to the children of men. Let them sacrifice the sacrifices of thanksgiving, and declare His works with rejoicing" (Psalms 107: 21-22 NKJV).*

Mary thanked the Lord for being chosen to carry the son of God. *"And Mary said, My soul magnifies the Lord, and my spirit has rejoiced in God my Savior. For He who is mighty has done great things for me, and Holy is His name" (Luke 1:46-47;49 NKJV).* Hannah thanked the Lord because God granted her petition to become pregnant with Samuel. *"So it came to pass in the process of time that Hannah conceived and bore a son, and called his name Samuel, saying, because I have asked for him from the Lord" (1 Samuel 1:20 NKJV). "And Hannah prayed and said, My heart rejoices in the Lord; My horn is exalted in the Lord. I smile at my enemies, because I rejoice in Your salvation" (1 Samuel 2:1 NKJV).* When you adopt the prayer of thanksgiving it will eventually usher you into the very presence of God. *"You will show me the path of life; In your presence is fullness of joy; at your right hand are pleasures forevermore" (Psalm 16:11 NKJV).*

THE PRAYER OF INTERCESSION

Interceding during prayer is a priority for any woman of God. Intercession is simply prayer to God, but with the focus being on behalf of another person. Even now, Jesus is still very active on our behalf in heaven interceding for us to the Father. *"It is Christ who died, and furthermore is also risen, who is even at the right hand of God, who also makes intercession for us" (Romans 8:31 NKJV).* The love of Christ truly amplifies through this verse of scripture. For He died for our sins, risen once again, seated at the right hand of God and working to reconcile us back to the Father through his prayer of intercession. How beautiful and powerful the agape love of God. The unconditional love of the Father who gave His only son to save us from eternal damnation. *"Therefore He is also able to save to the uttermost those who come to God through Him, since He always lives to make intercession for them" (Hebrews 7:25 NKJV).* You and I are constantly on the mind of Christ, as He lives to plead our case to the Father.

Since Jesus modeled the example of what intercession looks like, understand there are people in your life that could benefit from your personal time of intercession. Whether it's a child, spouse, sibling, parent, friend, or whomever, it is necessary to bring them before the Lord as He leads you to intercede on their behalf. Even Job through all his pain, suffering and losing everything, had found enough strength to pray for his friends. *"And the Lord restored Job's losses when he prayed for his friends. Indeed the Lord gave Job twice as much as he had before" (Job. 42.:10 NKJV)*. What a great example of the power of intercession and the unselfishness to consider others. Your breakthrough moment could manifest at any time when we just like Job, learn to pray for others even if we are suffering personal loss. Always be willing to intercede.

THE PRAYER OF DELIVERANCE

When you consider the word deliverance within the body of Christ; it's normally regarded as a very unpopular, unfamiliar word not accepted by religious people. Many have come to believe that deliverance only involves someone who has been possessed by a demon or under the influence of demonic control. Even though this is partially true, deliverance is not simply for demonized people, deliverance is for any and every one that desires to be rescued or set free.

The love of Christ often compelled Him to heal, deliver and set people free that were bound by demonic oppression. *"Then one was brought to Him who was demon-possessed, blind and mute; and He healed him, so that the blind and mute man both spoke and saw" (Matthew 12:22 NKJV). "Now there was a man in their synagogue with an unclean spirit and he cried out. But Jesus rebuked him, saying, be quiet and come out of him. And when the unclean spirit had convulsed him and cried out with a loud voice, he came out" (Mark 1:23;25-26 NKJV)*. Obviously, these verses of scripture are two examples where Christ had to come face to face with demon-possessed people. He had the power and authority to set the captives free.

As a woman of God you carry the same power and authority to command deliverance over your life as well as the lives of others. If we desire to see the prayer of deliverance manifest we must return to the stronghold of God. *(Zechariah 9:11-12 NKJV) says, "As for you also, Because of the blood of your covenant, I will set your prisoners free from the waterless pit. Return to the stronghold, You prisoners of hope. Even today I declare that I will restore double to you."* The stronghold of God is the shelter of God, a place of freedom for the believer. It's a spiritual fortress in Christ where we can dwell safely from the attacks of the devil while sheltered from the assignment of the destroyer. *"The Lord is my rock and my fortress in whom I take refuge; my shield and my stronghold" (Psalms 18:2 NKJV).*

The woman with the issue of blood suffered for twelve years with constant bleeding. According to the law in (Leviticus 15:25-27 NKJV), her issue qualified her as unclean. Whatever she sits on shall be unclean and whoever touches those things shall be unclean. Yet, regardless of her issue of blood; she decided to return to the stronghold of God. She had suffered many things from many physicians and spent all her money and was no better, but rather grew worse. *"When she heard about Jesus, she came behind Him in the crowd and touched His garment" (Mark 5:27 NKJV).*

Her willingness to touch was birthed from her desire to change. She simply made up her mind. *"For she said, If only I may touch His clothes, I shall be made well. Immediately the fountain of her blood was dried up, and she felt in her body that she was healed of the affliction" (Mark 5:28-29 NKJV).* Just like the woman with the issue of blood you may very well feel unclean, unholy, unrighteous and the enemy has convinced you that you will never be delivered from your condition. The devil is a liar! Stay encouraged my sister for deliverance is and will always be the children's bread. When the power had gone out of Jesus, He realized that He had been touched. He looked around to see her and He finally said to the women, *"Daughter, your faith has made you well. Go in peace, and be healed of your affliction" (Mark 5:34 NKJV).*

Therefore, I leave you with this salutation. As a woman of God, continue on your journey of developing a deeper life of prayer with our Heavenly Father. Always entering into His gates with thanksgiving and into His courts with praise. Remain steadfast, immovable, and always abounding in the work of the Lord by interceding for others knowing that your labor is not in vain. Finally, be strong in the Lord and in the power of His might. Make sure to put on the whole armor of God, that you may be able to stand against the wiles of the devil. Praying always with all prayer and supplication in the Spirit, being watchful to this end with all perseverance and knowing that deliverance is your portion.

Below is a sample prayer that you can follow as a guide as you are led in prayer by the Holy Spirit.

Dear Heavenly Father, and in the name of Jesus, I enter into your gates with thanksgiving and into your courts with praise. I am thankful unto You and bless Your Holy and righteous name. You alone are worthy, and so worthy to be praised! I come before you humbly as I know how to ask for your forgiveness. I repent of all of my sins because your Word says that if I confess my sins, you are faithful and just to forgive me and to cleanse me from all unrighteousness. I am truly grateful that I am the apple of your eye, fearfully and wonderfully made. For I am your workmanship, created in Christ Jesus for good works. As I intercede and stand in the gap on behalf of my family members, friends, neighbors, etc., I ask that you would heal, protect, and deliver them from all of their fears, calamities, sickness and diseases. For you are Jehovah Rapha, the Lord who heals physical and emotional wounds. Your Word says that by Your stripes, we are healed. Lord, I thank you that I can look toward the hills, because I know that my help comes from the Lord, the creator of heaven and earth. As I go forth in this new day, I thank you Lord for keeping your angels charge over me and for supernaturally delivering me. Now, in the Name of Jesus, I rebuke and come against any demonic or unclean spirit that would seek to torment my mind, body, or soul, and I plead the shed blood of Jesus over my mind, body, and soul right now in Jesus's Name. I now release the fruit of the Holy Spirit to take residence in my life. Lord, pour out Your spirit and use me for Your glory. Holy Spirit lead me in the way that I should go and give me the boldness to testify about Your love, goodness, mercy, and grace to those who need to experience Your transforming power in their lives in the mighty name of Jesus, Amen and Amen.

Pastor Elizabeth R. Butler is the spiritual daughter of Pastor Crystal Harrison. She is an anointed Woman of God who flows in the gifts of the Holy Spirit through healing and deliverance. Pastor Liz, as she is affectionately called, has been active in ministry for over 18 years. A true intercessor at heart, she carries a deep burden for God's people to return to their first love which is Jesus Christ through evangelizing the lost. Pastor Liz functions powerfully under the anointing and fire of the Holy Spirit through the gift of prophecy and as a prophetic dreamer. She strongly believes that healing is the children's bread and that all believers should be steadfast, unmovable, and always abounding in the work of the Lord. She has been happily married for 18 wonderful years to Alexander L. Butler. Together, they have four children, Caleb, Gabrielle, Juan, and Avanda. They currently reside in New Kent, Va.

Contact: info@apostolicpowerministries.com
Facebook: Elizabeth Spence Butler

Chapter Two- Elder Carla Smith

The Love of God

Born a coal-miner's daughter in rural Pennsylvania, and into a family of nine siblings, who would have thought that anything good could come out of such a small place. Oh, but wait, isn't that what they said about Jesus? Could anything good come out of Nazareth?

My name is Elder Carla J. Smith, married to Bishop Stanley K. Smith, retired Pastor of St. John Missionary Full Gospel Baptist Church and former Pennsylvania State Bishop of the Full Gospel Baptist Church Fellowship International. I am a wife, mother, grandmother, worker, leader, teacher, military veteran, First Lady, and ordained clergy. We have three adult daughters and five grandchildren. Being framed by culture, community, family, and friends, I was living life to the best of my ability. However, over time, I learned that my best was as filthy rags compared to what God had in store for me. God's love, grace and mercy had changed the trajectory of my life and afforded me the opportunity to wear many hats with the ability to minister to hundreds of women across the state of PA and stand before hundreds on international platforms.

While serving with many hats, I learned to multi-task, take what I hear with a grain of salt, and most importantly, with the help of God, I learned, and am still learning, about love. In each stage of hat wearing, it has taught me about love: how to look beyond faults and see a need, how to embrace the lovely and the unlovely, and how to be patient when it comes to receiving love in return. God's love is amazing. Some would say, love is complicated, but is it? I will admit that love is challenging, but not complicated or impossible because all things are possible with God. In this chapter, I will share what I discovered about God's love, its biblical definition, and why we are commanded to share God's love with others. Receiving and understanding God's love will not only change you, but it will change the trajectory of your life.

The Love of God

Love is a force that has the ability to change us all

Love, this 4-letter word, is powerful and is a force that seeks the welfare of all and has the ability to change us all. It is a very familiar word that is used quite often by many, especially those of us who are Christians. Love is universal. It is spoken in every language and its reach is around the world. The bible tells us to love one another. It tells us that *"For God so loved the world that He gave his only begotten Son. That whosoever believeth in Him should not perish, but have everlasting life."* St. John 3:16. *"Greater love hath no man than this, than a man lay down his life for his friends."* And, *"As the Father hath loved me, so have I loved you, continue ye in my love."* John 15:9.

We are told to love, but do we know how? Do we know what love really mean? Can you define love? If so, how would you define it? What would you say? If several people were to write down their definition of love, I believe there would be different definitions of what love is. Do we fully understand love? How do we continue in His love when we haven't come to the understanding of what love is?

Merriam-Webster defines love as:

> **1a (1):** strong affection for another arising out of kinship or personal ties
> **(2):** attraction based on sexual desire : affection and tenderness felt by lovers **(3):** affection based on admiration, benevolence, or common interests **b:** an assurance of affection **2:** warm attachment, enthusiasm, or devotion **3a:** the object of attachment, devotion, or admiration **b(1):** a

beloved person : <u>Darling</u> —often used as a term of endearment **(2)** *British* —used as an informal term of address **4a:** unselfish loyal and benevolent concern for the good of another: such as **(1):** the fatherly concern of God for humankind **(2):** brotherly concern for others **b:** a person's adoration of God **5:** a god (such as Cupid or Eros) or <u>personification</u> of love **6:** an <u>amorous</u> episode : <u>love</u> affair **7:** the sexual embrace : <u>Copulation</u> [intercourse] **8:** a score of zero, to hold dear : <u>Cherish</u>: to feel a lover's passion, devotion, or tenderness for, <u>Caress</u>: to fondle amorously, to copulate with, to like or desire actively : take pleasure in, to <u>thrive</u> in, to feel affection or experience desire **9** *capitalized, Christian Science* : <u>GOD</u>

Merriam-Webster made a great attempt in defining the word love. Most would agree with Webster's definition because that is what we've been taught. Webster is not incorrect in its definition; however, it is incomplete in its definition. The reason we struggle in the area of love is because there are too many definitions. When it comes to love, people expect different things. Some desire touch, some words of affirmation, some by giving gifts, and the list goes on and on, often missing the mark because we have not met each other's definition of love. Instead of coming together, we grow apart due to irreconcilable differences. Different perspectives can end up in divorce, children run away from home, and people drift apart. Could this be the result of a mere misunderstanding of the definition of love? People are looking for others to meet their expectation of love. If we can find a biblical definition of love, it is hopeful that people could come together, stay together, and receive and release love the way God intended.

Webster's definition did not say, "love is a Spirit", nor did it say, "love is unconditional", nor did it say, "love is power", nor did it say, "love is sacrificial", nor did it say, "love is Agape", nor did it say, "love is the first fruit of the Holy Spirit". Webster defines love as a feeling or desire. It describes the effects of love or the outcome of love and not the true essence of love. We use the word love loosely to describe things, such as, I love my house, I love pizza, or I love a certain color, etc., but how does the bible use the word love? I John 4:7-8 states *"Beloved, let us love one another: for love is of God; and every one that loveth is born of God, and knoweth God. He that loveth not knoweth not God; for God is love."* The bible also states in John 4:24 *"**God is a Spirit**: and they that worship Him must worship Him in spirit and in truth."* If God is a Spirit, and God is Love, wouldn't that make love a Spirit? Trying to define love is like trying to define God. We can't because God's ways are not our ways nor are His thoughts our thoughts. God is infinite and we are finite. He is bigger than we could ever know or imagine.

The Spirit told me to stop trying to figure out God, you have to just know that you know that you know that He is. The same with love, we have to embrace it for what it is – Spiritual. Love is a Spirit, Love is God. That's why it's said in holy matrimony that *what God put together, let no man put asunder* and allow His Spirit, the Holy Spirit to work in the marriage. In other words, we must keep God at the center of the marriage and in relationships. It's Spiritual! If we could get a hold of this revelation, there would be less divorces, more families would stay together, more people would get along and there would be more harmony among the brethren; and genuine love would manifest.

Love is a Spirit

Love is a Spirit. To flow in love effectively you must be in the Spirit. Spend time with God. Spend time in God's Word - God and His Word are one. Spend time in prayer and meditate on God's Word. The bible says that *if you are in the Spirit, you will not fulfill the lust of the flesh.* Being in the Spirit, you will begin to understand the things of the Spirit, comparing spiritual things with spiritual (I Cor. 2:13). Divine revelation takes place in the Spirit. The flesh must decrease daily so that the Spirit in you can live. Paul said, *"for me to live is Christ, and to die is gain."* If the Spirit in you live – then love in you will abound. I Corinthians 13 says, *"And now abideth, faith, hope, and charity; these three; but the greatest of these is charity* (Love)." It clearly states that love is the greatest attribute we have and without love, what we do means nothing as it is like sounding brass and a tingling symbol. Love is the evidence of God's presence in our lives, for Jesus said, *"By this all men will know that you are my disciples, if you love one another."* John 13:35. God and Love are one. Love is the very character of God.

> *"For this is the message that ye heard from the beginning, that we should love one another. For we know that we have passed from death to life, because we love the brethren. Let us not love in word, neither in tongue, but in deed and in truth. Let us love one another for love is of God; and every one that loveth is born of God, and knoweth God. If we love one another, God dwelleth in us, and His love is perfected in us. God is love and he that dwelleth in love dwelleth in God and God in him. Herein is our love perfect, that we may have boldness in the day of judgment: because as He is, so are we in this world. There is no fear in love; but perfect love casteth out fear. We love Him because He first loved us. For this is the love of God that we keep His commandments... " Thou shalt love the Lord thy God with all thine heart, with all thy soul, with all thy mind, and with all thy strength, this is the first commandment. And the second is like unto it, thou shalt love thy neighbor as thyself." On theses*

> *two commandments hang all the law and the prophets."*

Love's Attributes

Sacrificial: *"For God so loved the world that He gave His only begotten Son, that whosoever believeth on Him should not perish, but have everlasting life:*" John 3:16. God showed the greatest love to humankind when He sent His Son Jesus to be the sacrifice for the sin of the entire world. This self-sacrificing love is the very foundation of Christianity.

The First Fruit of the Holy Spirit: Galatians 5, The fruit of the Spirit is *love, joy, peace, patience, kindness, generosity, faithfulness gentleness, and self-control.*

Love is the basis of the other fruit of the Spirit to manifest. You shall know a tree by its fruit. Jesus states that you will be able to identify false prophets by their fruit. False prophets will not produce good fruit. Fruit, which is a common metaphor in both the Old and New Testaments, represent the outward manifestation of a person's faith, thus their behavior and their works. God said to *be fruitful, and multiply, and replenish the earth.* Genesis 1:28: What fruit do you think He was talking about, multiplication of family? Yes, but could He be speaking about multiplication of bearing good fruit as well. *Oh, taste and see that the Lord is good* through the good fruit you bear. How can others taste and see that the Lord is good unless they see the good fruit in you?

Powerful: When God's love is demonstrated it has the ability and power to pull on the heartstrings of humankind. Keep in mind that God is Love and He is also Spirit, which makes Love a Spirit. And if Love is a Spirit, it has the ability to draw people into fellowship with God and with each other. Love demonstrates. Love can soften the heart with the ability to change us, if we allow it. That is the key, if we allow it. Knowing that God is Love and Love is God, can we also say:

> Love is Alpha and Omega, love it is the beginning and the end, love is kind, love envieth not, love vaunteth not itself, love is not puffed up, love forgives, love rejoiceth not in iniquity, love rejoiceth in truth, love hopeth all things, love endureth all things, love believeth all things, love thinketh

no evil, love is long-suffering, love is gentleness, love is temperance, love is genuine, love is true, love is a friend that sticks closer than a brother, love is everlasting, love never fails, love is patience, love is healing, love is restoration, love is unconditional, love is sacrificial, love looks beyond faults and sees the need, love comforts, love is freedom, love is power, love is humility, love is a Spirit, and Love is God?

Unconditional: God separates the person from the issue and never separates us from His love. There is nothing we can do that will stop God's love for us. After all, while we were yet sinners, Christ died for us. The bible says, *"Who shall separate us from the love of Christ? Shall tribulation, or distress, or persecution, or famine, or nakedness, or peril, or sword? For I am persuaded, that neither death, nor life, nor angels, nor principalities, nor powers nor things present, nor things to come, nor height, nor depth, nor any other creature, shall be able to separate us from the love of God, which is in Christ Jesus our Lord."* Nothing can separate us from the love of God because God's love is unconditional.

Different Stages of Love

According to Kenneth S. Wuest, there are four words in the Greek language for love (1988).

1. **Storge** (*Stergein*) – Natural affection in one's own nature as between a mother and a child

2. **Eros** (*Eran*) – Sensual or passion love.

3. **Phileo** (*Philein*) – Friendship or brotherly love. Gives love, but expects something in return.

4. **Agape'**(*Agapan/Agapao*) – Sacrificial unconditional love. Totally unselfish. The love that keeps on giving without expecting anything in return. This is the ultimate love that we

all strive for. Love without any strings attached. This is the love that God releases, and it is life changing.

There are different stages of love. Each stage of love builds on the other. They are interrelated so that the physical, emotional, and spiritual processes overlap and reinforce each other in the act of loving. Needless-to-say, no matter what stage, love is still a Spirit, and that Spirit is of God and imparted into us by God.

The Greatest Commandment

"And thou shalt love the Lord thy God with all thy heart, and with all thy soul, and with all thy mind, and with all thy strength, this is the first commandment. And the second is like unto it, love thy neighbor as thyself" Mark 12:30-31

Love is the leading affection of the soul; the love of God is the leading grace in the renewed soul (Bible Study Tools, 2022). We love God because He first loved us. When we truly love God with all our heart, soul, mind, and strength, our actions will display it and others will notice. They will see the results of what love produces. The kingdom agenda will always include others and will always work on behalf of someone else. God's love and anointing is not just for you and your four and no more. His anointing is released when His will, plan and purpose is being fulfilled, which is meeting the needs of the people, and loving the people. How can we say we love God who we have not seen and hate our brother who we have seen? If so, we lie and the truth is not in us. (I John 4:20)

All of Christianity comes down to how we love God and how everything we do in relationships, work, education, entertainment, serving in ministry, etc., displays our love for God. No success, college degrees, status, or what we own, will matter at the end of our days. How we loved God and loved others will be our victory (Bible Study Tools, 2022). If you desire to see God's kingdom agenda manifest in your life and in the communities in which you reside, release

God's love to those around you, and watch God do great and mighty things through you and among His people.

Ask God for More God

We ask God for material things, i.e., cars, houses, clothes, jobs, more money, we ask for husbands or wives, we ask for more anointing, more power, more gifts, more glory, more, more, more. What if we ask God for more God? Ask God to decrease you and increase Him in your life. John the Baptist said, *"I must decrease that He may increase."* If we ask God for more God – He will impart more God. If He imparts more God, He imparts more LOVE. If He imparts more Love, He imparts more power, and we will be able to flow in all that God is. If we want to operate in the full power of God, we must begin to major in the minor and/or master the minor, which is really the major – LOVE, the mere essence of God.

Love is God and love is a Spirit. Jesus taught us and demonstrated His love through His sacrificial offering on the cross. Through His death, burial, and resurrection, we have been redeemed and bought with a price. Through the process of time, and accepting Christ into my life, God's love changed me into the woman of God that I am today. My prayer is that you receive this gift of love by accepting Jesus into your life as your personal Lord and Savior. And, whatever hat you wear, you will be able to pass His love on to others. Can anything good come out of a small town in Pennsylvania? If God is in it, absolutely yes!

Contact: http://www.anointedvesselbooks.com

Chapter Three- Helen Bowman
The Friendship of God

The Bible tells us that *"A friend loves at all times and a brother is born for a time of adversity." (Proverbs 17:17 NKJV) "My command is this: Love each other as I have loved you. Greater love has no one than this; to lay down one's life for one's friends." "This is My commandment, that you love one another as I have loved you. Greater love has no one than this, than to lay down one's life for his friends. You are my friends if you do whatever I command you. No longer do I call you servants, for a servant does not know what his master is doing; but I have called you friends, for all things that I heard from My Father I have made known to you." (John 15:12-15 (NKJV).*

After reading these scriptures, a thought came to mind, what does being a friend to God look like. I will share three points about what this could look like. There are others, but I will only share these three:

1. **To be able to listen to God, to watch what we see or hear, where we go, what we think, who we trust, and what we do.**

Do we go into our secret closet and call out to Him and wait to hear what He has to say, or do we rush in and out as a duty? As a friend of God, are we doing what is pleasing to Him or are we doing what feels good to us? As we do with our earthly friends, sharing, spending time with them, waiting for advice, trusting them with our secrets and desires, God desires the same from us, to communicate and share things with us. "For Jesus, friendship is the ultimate relation-ship with God and one another." (Gail R. O'Day) *Jeremiah 33:3 (NKJV) says, "Call to Me, and I will answer you, and show you great and mighty things, which you do not know."* God has things He wants us to know, but if we are not friends with Him, you might not ever know. Also, He says in *Jeremiah 29:11-13 (NKJV), "For I know the thoughts that I think toward you, says the LORD, thoughts of peace and not of evil, to give you a future and a hope. Then you will call upon Me and go and pray to Me, and I will listen to you. And you will seek Me and find Me, when you search for Me with all your heart."*

There were times when I had to call out to God because of some personal issues I faced. At the time, I was not ready to share some of my feelings with my earthly friends, or my situation because of what I thought they would say, what they would think of me, are they going to judge me, would they want to know, like Job's friend, what did I do to cause this, so I took the issues to God. With God being my friend, He placed me in a holding place where no one could bother me. I was there, just God and me, and He gave me hope and He comforted me to the point that as to this day, I do not know or remember what all I went through. With God being my friend and comforter, He took the pain instead of me, He took the shame off me, He placed me in the crook of His shoulder and kept me there until He knew I could manage it. Also, during this time, He placed wonderful people in my life, ones I could physically talk with, laugh with, cry if I needed to. These friends sent me CDs to help comfort me, prayed with and for me, gave gifts to cheer me up, and talked with me no matter what time of day or night it was. They were there all the time. Right now, I do not see them often or talk with them weekly, but we share a close friendship that God orchestrated! God cares so much for us that He takes the pain that we go through and placed it upon himself when He went to the cross to die for each of us.

There is a song called, "He Was There All the Time," sung by The Sensational Nightingale and Rev. James Moore. It goes like this:

> *"...When I felt like giving up*
> *He was there all the time*
> *He was there all the time*
> *Waiting patiently in light*
> *He was there all the time.*
>
> *...He was there*
> *Heeee was there*
> *May times I tried to do it on my own*
> *Realized that after a while all of my strength was gone*
> *Ohhh nobody was around*
> *I called my family*
> *Some of them couldn't be found*
> *That's why I had to depend on Jesus*
> *I had to lean on Him*
> *I had to call on Him*
> *I had to bend down on my knees*
> *And He answered my prayer*
> *Can I get a witness?"*

Are we listening to God to find out what He has to say, for His correction and advice and then follow His instructions? In *Proverbs*

8:32-36 (ESV), it says, "And now, O sons, listen to me: blessed are those who keep my ways. Hear instruction and be wise, and do not neglect it. Blessed is the one who listens to me, watching daily at my gates, waiting beside my doors. For whoever finds me finds life and obtains favor from the LORD, but he who fails to find me injures himself; all who hate me love death."

"Jesus gave everything to his friends – his knowledge
of God and his own life.
Jesus is our model for friendship because
he loved without limits and he makes it possible for us
to live a life of friendship
because we have been transformed
by everything he shared with us."
Gail R. O'Day

2. Are we making ourselves available to get close to God? You might ask, "How can we spend time with God?"

We can spend time with God by getting into His Word, attending Bible studies, fellowshipping with like-minded believers, going to church/fellowships, and have an active prayer life. Are we doing these things because we desire to be close to God or are we delighting in His Word to get something from Him? *Psalm 37:4 (ESV), it says, "Delight yourself in the LORD, and he will give you the desires of your heart."* When we delight in something, we enjoy it to its fullest. Just like when we get with our friends and have time for them, laughing and talking, do we do this with God? God wants us to enjoy our time with Him as well. God loves for us to share with him how our day is going, what is on our mind, what is going right or wrong in our day, etc. God wants to know and be in every aspect of our lives. We can talk to our friends for hours on end. So can we say if we are a friend of Jesus, how much time we spend with Him getting to know His heart and His desires for us.

God does reward us, but that should not be our only goal, to get Him to do something for us. In *Psalm 147:11(NKJV), "The LORD takes pleasure in those who fear Him, In those who hope in His mercy."*

3. **Do we have a loving relationship with God and love Him with all our heart? God's love for us is uncondi-tional.**

He loves us no matter what we have done, where we have been, or have plans to do. He desires to have a loving relationship with us. In *Matthews 22:37 (NLT), it says, "Jesus replied, "You must love the LORD your God with all your heart, all your soul, and all your mind."* You must have love in your heart to love another person. You put your friend's needs over yours. God's love for us showed when His son died on the cross for our sins. God loved us so much that He laid down His life for us. God's love is a fatherly love. In *1 John 3:1 (NKJV), it says, "Behold what manner of love the Father has bestowed on us, that we should be called children of God."* God places this love in our hearts so that we can love others as He loves us and command us to do the same. We can also win others to God by the love we have for God.

There was another time that I stood on the Word of God and contin-ued to love someone that did not love me. It was hard, but with God all things are possible. I had to stand with God, and He with me, to get through this time as well. In the end, God showed that by loving Him, trusting Him, having faith, that love conquers all. It shows in our friendship and relationships with others. We can ask ourselves; do we love God more than we love ourselves or others. However, we know the answer. God does command us to love Him as well as others. *1 Corinthians 13:4-5 (NIV), says: "Love is patient, love is kind. It does not envy, it does not boast, it is not proud. It does not dishonor others, it is not self-seeking, it is not easily angered, it keeps no record of wrongs."*

Will we choose friendship with God or the ways of the world? Will we seek out the one who is our creator, who loves us unconditionally, who is LORD of LORDS, King of Kings, our one true God! In *Revelation 3:20 (NKJV), it says, "Behold, I stand at the door and knock. If anyone hears My voice and opens the door, I will come into him and dine with him, and he with Me."*

In summary, with being in a friendship with God, do we watch what we say, what we see and do, where we go, who we associate with, what books we read, what movies we go to, who we enter into our homes and if certain people come to our homes, do we have to clear our coffee table of things that should not be there. There is a song that comes to mind from Sunday School, "Be Careful Little Eyes What You See, For the Father up above is looking down in love, so be careful of the things you see, hear, do, say..." Extend these to your children, spouse, and friends. Separate yourself from what the world is doing and focus on what the LORD has commanded you to do. "To keep Jesus' commandment is to enact his love in our own lives. Jesus affirms the significance of this commandment by stating that his followers become his friends to the extent that they keep his commandments." (Gail R. O'Day)

James 4:4 (NKJV), says, "… Do you know that friendship with the world is enmity with God? Whoever therefore wants to be a friend of the world makes himself an enemy of God."

If we say God hears and sees everything that we do, ask ourselves would God be pleased for what He sees us do, places we go, what we say and think, how we treat our spouses and children, are we pleased with the job, finances, and homes he has entrusted to us.

"Jesus gave everything to his friends—his knowledge of God and his own life. Jesus is our model for friendship—because he loved without limits— and he makes it possible for us to live a life of friendship—because we have been transformed by everything he shared with us. Through friendship we come to know God and through friendship we enact the love of God. We can risk being friends because Jesus has been a friend to us." (Gail R. O'Day)

God wants us to stay close to Him and take all our cares to Him. Remember that Jesus says that "He is always there for us and that we can cast all our cares on Him because He cares for us." Our earthly friends could be there with us only for a season; however, God is there for eternity. God places them there for us because he knows what we need and when we need it. God is in our lives orchestrating every jot or tittle and He knows what is best for us.

Supporting information taken from:

"I Have Called You Friends", Gail R. O'Day, 2008.

Internet, "What Jesus Say About Friendship With Him"

Helen Bowman was born and reared in James City County, Virginia. She is the daughter of the late Samuel T. and Lucy Ellen Jones. She has eight brothers and sisters with two deceased sisters.

Helen attended Williamsburg/James City County Public Schools and graduated from Bruton Height School in 1966. She graduated from Christopher Newport University in 1978, with a BS in Business Administration. In 2002, she completed the Alternative Route to Teacher Education Program from Hampton University. She was a Home Visitor for the Williamsburg/James City County Head Start Program for four years and for six years was their Education Specialist. After leaving Head Start, she worked and retired from Charles City County Public Schools, after working there for almost fifteen years as a Preschool Teacher, Kindergarten Teacher, and a Reading Teacher.

Helen is a divorcee and is the proud mother of four wonderful adult children, Tonya, Marcia, Brian, and Michael and eleven impressive grandchildren.

She is an active member of The Historic First Baptist Church of Williamsburg, Virginia, where she is a member of Shekinah Glory Praise Dancers, plays with The Historic First Baptist Church Bell Choir, and teaches Sunday School. She is an active member of The Eagle Network Worldwide and serves on the Board of "Time-Out!" Outreach Ministry. She is active in her community and serves as the President of The Greater Williamsburg Women's Association and is a Board Member of The Virginia State Literacy Association.

Helen is believer in the Word of God and that God is the head of her life. While completing a Bible Study with her Shekinah Glory Praise Dancers called "Praying The Names of God," she realized these many names of God is helping to navigate her life every day and that makes God closer to her and is the reason she can say we are a friend of God, and that God is our friend. Through her struggles, she has been standing many years on *Jeremiah 29:11, "For I know the thoughts that I think toward you, says the LORD, thoughts of peace and not of evil, to give you a future and a hope."*

Contact: helenbowman48@gmail.com

Chapter Four- Margaret Marie Ware

The Heart of God

Proverbs 3:5 "Trust in the Lord with all your heart and lean not on your own understanding."

As I began to write this chapter, I realized what a difficult time I was having. I must have started this chapter three or four different times. I deal with a lot of things and wear many hats every day. I have a loving husband that takes care of me well. I care for my ill mother who I promised I wouldn't put in a nursing home because people are so cruel and uncaring. I do the best I can helping to take care of the church in which I belong and to top it all dealing with people with different personalities I never know what's going to come at me one way or the other.

But through all this and some I had to grow up to know some things. People can be and are at times very nasty, mean, and impatient, which at times if you're not careful you can fall into that same pattern.

Getting involved with all kinds of things like selling and doing drugs, selling my body, stripping and much more, my mind was leading me down a road of destruction, yet I've always had and still have love and compassion.

Life was not always easy as a mother of 4 children, 2 different fathers with barely any help. Many days I felt suicidal and at night left in the dark crying some of the biggest tears you could ever imagine. I've walked in FEAR (false evidence appearing real) for most of my life so writing this is a good challenge for me.

I've always been a big push over because of an inner weakness. As a child, the people I grew up with used to call me black and ugly and to get them to like me I would take the money that I earned doing hair and spend it on them. There was a season in my life where I wanted to give my children away with the condition that they all stay together. I went to my pastor at the time, and he suggested that I rethink what I wanted to do. I'm glad I didn't make that move of giving them away because they are the gift that God gave to me, and we are closer now than ever before. God kept me and I didn't know that it was Him. I thought it was me thinking smarter.

I can't thank God enough for showing me His love and affection that I haven't always shown to others. The Heart of God is in our best interest. What concerns us concerns God. Because our thoughts are not His thoughts and our ways are not His ways, we are very blessed to have God as our lookout because we can't see everything. We need to learn that if we don't know how to trust Him to not be afraid to talk to Him. It's okay to cry to Him and tell Him how you feel. He understands your hurt and joy. He knows what you need when you need it. Give your faith a job to do while you work (any kind of work) during the day and rest and sleep at night.

There will be times when you will walk alone because you can't take everyone with you where you're going. He sees and knows your efforts.

HEART- The heart is the Locus of physical and spiritual being and represents the central wisdom of feeling as opposed to the head. Wisdom of reason. It is compassion and understanding, life giving and complex. It is a symbol for love. Often known as the seat of emotions, the heart is synonymous with affection.
PURE HEART- Jesus says "pure in heart" which is referring to internal purity, once again, showing His concern with our hearts position. Jesus doesn't waste time speaking to our external lives because He knows that our hearts must first be changed.

My God, My God, My God!!!!!!!
When I think of the heart of God, I think of you and I, and how He had us in His mind long before we were conceived in our mother's womb. Then I think of His Word which is indeed His heart. I think of big love, agape love, viscous love, more love than I could ever imagine, give, or show.

That's why He's God and His heart is the way it is. No persons' heart can compare to God's heart. God's heart is so big and great that He created a world to worship Him and yet He doesn't force us to do so. God is a gentleman!!!

The heart of God is the strongest of any heart I know.
The heart of God makes us different. It leads, guides, strengthens and keeps us all.

The heart of God puts us in a place of peace, helps us to speak when needed and to be quiet as well. The heart of God teaches us to praise Him, be thankful and pray continually to Him. His heart permits the sun to shine through the clouds to give us light so we can continue to see what we can't.

The heart of God brings us out of our toughest situations without us realizing it and yet He allows us to live through it. (Some of us are still going through some things we need to get out of). His heart teaches us how to show ourselves friendly to others and to be firm when needed. The heart of God is gentle, kind, reliable and fair. His heart also knows how to discipline and chastise and yet still love unconditionally.

According to them (the people I grew up with) I never amounted to anything even to this day, but I've always liked them, I really cared about them. I wanted so badly to be a part of the clique they were in, but I didn't measure up no matter what I did. That still happens to this very day with people I deal with on a regular basis (ignoring them doesn't always work).

I've been raped, been made to walk the streets naked, beaten, bones broken, talked about, mistreated and abused regularly; yet my heart said forgive and love even though I didn't know what true forgiveness or love was at that time.

In my life, my heart has been broken more times than a $20,000 VASE (LOL). Don't get me wrong, I've had some good times and seasons in my life as well. When I got saved at 15 years old, when I gave birth to my children, when I got married to my first and second husbands and many, many more times and events. Those were some of the most enjoyable moments in my life.

Here you'll find that in our lifetime we've done a lot of things that we're not so proud of but God, Oh God through His big heart saw fit to spare us. The heart of God feels pain and agony when we are disobedient, disrespectful, rebellious, nasty, and mean. It hurts Him. If we could love and care half as much as He does we really would be doing something.

When God made a woman, He gave us many loving attributes. Although we are all different, He gave women a part of His heart because He knew we would need and must have it. We as women carry the heart of God. We have compassion, love, forgiveness, nurturing, care, concern, reasoning, understanding, sometimes tough love, anger, punishment and much more.

I see that God trusts women with a lot of His personal heart because He knows that with His help we will get the job done and we'll keep going with it because it's beneficial.

The heart of God is the essence of who He is, what He desires, His will and His purpose, God's heart is full of nutrients. God is A Gentleman.

As I was writing, I realized that I'm really outdated with a lot of things. Then God came along and answered my prayers. I prayed for new, different, trustworthy, God fearing, loving friends. It gets lonely sometimes not having anyone to talk to or cry to or laugh with because I always wanted to be called and considered special without having to work so hard just to hear that. But that's not my primary goal of mine. My gifts make room for me and therefore I am special in God's eyes because He made me that way.

I've been in some very low places in my life but at my very lowest, the God I serve never once let me touch the ground. He was always there to catch me, cushion my fall and protect me. Now that's the Heart of God!!!

Here are some scriptures that I believe would help you to get your heart lined up with God's heart.

Mathew 6:21- For where your treasure is, there your heart will be also.
Before you give someone your heart you must determine the condition of theirs.

Proverbs 3:5-Trust in the Lord with all your heart and lean not on your own understanding. Include God in everything you do, and this way you give Him a chance to keep you on the right track.

Proverbs 4:23- Above all else guard your heart for everything you do flows from it.

Elder Margaret Marie (Tammy) Ware is a wife, mother, grand-mother and Pastor. She has been married to Ronald Ware for almost 13 years. They have 9 children (1 deceased), and 19 grandchildren.

Elder Tammy is the Action Pastor (Yes, Action Pastor) of Anointed Full Gospel Methodist Church in Chester, PA. She ensures to the best of her ability that the church is still functioning and active since the illness of Senior Pastor, Margaret M. Benson. Elder Tammy was called by the Lord to serve in ministry 100 percent in 1989 and has been serving Him ever since. Her goals are to get souls saved, help provide a safe, trustworthy, non-threatening environment for people to be strengthened and grow in relationship with Jesus Christ.

Chapter Five- Carol A. Bryant

The Forgiveness of God

Forgiveness: The action or process of forgiving or being forgiven.

Forgiveness according to The Bible is correctly understood as God's promise not to count our sins against us.

We see the definitions of forgiveness but what does God's forgiveness look like? First, God's forgiveness is an expression of God's love, God Himself tells us in Exodus 34:7 "I lavish unfailing love to a thousand generations."

God's forgiveness is also an expression of God's grace. Ephesians 2-8, Peter 3, and Romans 3 and 6 are some chapters in The Bible that speak on this grace of God that flows from His forgiveness.

God's forgiveness is also an expression of His mercy. *Hebrews 4:16, "Let us therefore come boldly to the throne of grace that we may obtain mercy."*

God's forgiveness is also an expression of His generosity. *1 Timothy 6:17, "Command those who are rich in this present world not to be arrogant not to put their hope in wealth which is so uncertain but to put their hope in God who richly provides us with everything for our enjoyment."*

Forgiveness is the divine miracle of grace. The cost to God was the Cross of Christ. To forgive sin while remaining a Holy God this price had to be paid.

Forgiveness has always been God's plan. *Psalm 86:5, "You, Lord are forgiving and good, abounding in love to all who call to you."* Forgiveness is a gift: *Isaiah 55:6-7, "Seek The Lord while He may be found; call on Him while He is near."* And God allows the choice to accept His gift of forgiveness.

Matthew 26:28, "This is my blood of the covenant, which is poured out for many for the forgiveness of sins." God's forgiveness cannot be lost (Ephesians 1:7) but we must confess our sins (1 John 1:9). There is importance of repentance in light of God's forgiveness.

(Acts 3:19 – Acts 10:43) Hope and peace in Christ is rooted in God's forgiveness and God's forgiveness is reciprocal.

(Ephesians 4:32), "Be kind and compassionate to one another, forgiving each other just as in Christ, God forgave you." We are all in need of forgiveness from God, we all have committed sin. (Eccl. 7:20) If we claim we have no sin we deceive ourselves and the truth is not in us because all sin is an act of rebellion against God. (Psalm 51:4) So as a result we desperately need God's forgiveness.

So how do we open our spirit to receive God's forgiveness? We all long to know we are loved, accepted, and forgiven. The scriptures promise that God will not reject us when we come to Him with broken and contrite hearts. There is peace, joy, freedom, and victory to our lives through the forgiveness of God. Thankfully, God is loving, merciful and eager to forgive us our sins. (2 Peter 3:9) God provides for our forgiveness. Hallelujah! Jesus died on the cross taking the penalty that we deserved – Death. (2 Corinthians 5:21) God provided forgiveness for the sins of the entire world. 1 John 2:2 proclaims, *"In Jesus we have redemption through His blood, the forgiveness of sins in accordance with the riches of God's grace."*

We are to forgive others and let God move. Our greatest example of forgiveness comes from Jesus! Jesus taught us the importance and power of forgiveness and He too had to forgive those who mistreated Him and those who crucified Him. At the cross He said, *"Father forgive them for they do not know what they do (Luke 23:34).* The Power of God's forgiveness is evident when we choose to forgive out offenders. When we forgive others, we free ourselves from the power others have over us.

The Word is clear that God expects us to forgive as many times as we need to. *"Peter came to Jesus and asked, "Lord, how many times shall I forgive my brother or sister who sins against me? Up to seven times?" Jesus answered, "I tell you not seven times but seventy-seven times" (Matthew 18:21-22).* In The Bible this includes forgiving everyone every time of everything as an act of obedience and gratefulness to God. It acknowledges the sacrifice God made through His son Jesus who died to restore the relationship between God and man. The beauty of The Bible is the "good news" that God forgives those who confess their sins by repenting (turning away) with humbleness.

Forgiving doesn't mean we forget, just that we surrender the hurt to God. Choose not to hold it against the person. There is freedom in releasing. You may still remember but pray that your heart will not hold onto anger when you remember it. The offender may already be living free of the offense. People think that because they have forgiven someone that they have to instantly forget the offense but only God can do that. That is the forgiveness of God. *Isaiah 43:25, "I, even I, am He who blots out your transgressions for my own sake and remembers your sins no more."*

Forgiveness is who God is. It is His nature. That is what He does! He is willing and ready to forgive any inequity (sin) and any rebellion. He is a God of forgiveness. Once you have experienced the forgiveness of God you are then able to forgive others. *Colossians 3:13, "Bearing with one another and forgiving one another."*

The Bible is one long story of how God reaches out to show His love and forgiveness toward us (mankind). In Genesis 3:15, God gives His first promise of a Redeemer who would forgive the world of their sin.

The Bible gives various stories demonstrating forgiveness of God.

God's forgiveness is a story of our salvation from the beginning of time, in the first pages of scripture; God called us "very good" and had a plan in place to save us. Not an account of what we could ever do or accomplish, but of who He is and what He would do. We are His. This curse of sin won't last forever. Jesus has already defeated death, the curtain has been torn, and we have been forgiven.

For all who declare Jesus as savior and confess their sin, eternity awaits.

Jesus will return. Amen.

Carol A. Bryant is a wife, mother of two sons, grandmother of three, and the eldest of three siblings. She has worked in the fields of healthcare and education.

She is a daughter of The Most High God.

carolbryant14@yahoo.com

Chapter Six- Sabrina Clemons

The Faith of God

Now Faith is the substance of things hoped for and the evidence of things not seen (Hebrews 11:1 KJV). But without faith it is impossible to please him; for he that cometh to God must believe that he is, and that he is a rewarder of them that diligently seek him. (Hebrew 11:6 KJV)

A true woman of God is truly a woman of *faith*. *Faith* is a foundational stone to the spiritual walk and growth in God. There is much that can be said about faith, but what is really the *faith* of God? Can it simply be said that the *faith* of God is actually *faith* IN God? If that is the case, what is *faith* in God? Well let's explore this. *Faith* is defined as a strong belief or trust in God, or complete confidence in someone or something. It can also be defined as a system of religious belief. There is a system of belief as it pertains to the Kingdom of God that sets us apart as true believers and Kingdom citizens. God's system of believing is not a "religious" act or duty, but it is actually a process of doing things the Kings way and according to his governing and His Word. It's believing that His Word is the truth. God's system is the only process that works and is right. He is not a man that He should or ever would lie. What God has spoken was and is to come.

As a child, I was often taught about *faith* and having faith in God. However, I still really did not know what it really meant until I had my own experiences in a walk of *faith* with the Lord. I was raised in the church and went religiously every week. Sunday church, Wednesday Bible study, and vacation Bible school was a requirement. My father was a Bible believer and dedicated much of his time teaching us the scripture. One of the first scriptures I learned and committed to memory from the Bible was *faith* comes by hearing, and hearing by the Word of God (Romans10:17 KJV). Although I learned that scripture, I did not understand the full context. I knew there was a God, and that He was the creator. I learned about His creation and the stories in the Old Testament. I also learned stories about Jesus Christ. I heard the weekly sermons. Although this all contributed to me knowing about this God of the Bible and the groundwork of believing in Him, I didn't know Him. I knew of God…. but I did not know God. However, seeds of *faith* were sown in the ground of my heart, and it was later that those seeds were watered by the Holy Spirit. Such has been the beginning stages in the faith of God for many believers. Being taught about God, seeing his creation and hearing of His word. Nevertheless, faith in God is a continual process of learning and experience. It is a journey. Enhancement in our faith of God involves relationship with Him and ultimately obedience. It involves learning of Him – who He is, His what, why and how. It not only involves believing, but it involves hoping and trusting, and having confidence that God will do what He says and that He will carry out His promises. As a kingdom citizen, I now have an even better understanding of what faith really is.

There are many examples in the Bible about the faith of God. There are two in particular that stands out to me as a woman of faith. One account is that of Sarah and Abraham. God told her husband that they were going to have a son. Sarah heard this and she laughed. The evidence for her was not there. She reached an old age and was childless. Yet God promised that Sarah would be of mother of many nations and that out of Abraham would come kings and many nations. God first visited Abraham and had a conversation with him, sharing his plan. God's plan included instructions. Abraham believed God. See, God and Abraham had a relationship. They walked and talked together. Abraham knew God and he believed whatever God said. However, Sarah's relationship with God was not quite the same. Although He told her that she would conceive a son, Sarah believed that she was too old. She did not have hope. From the time that God first told Abraham that he would have a son, some time had passed, and the son had not come to pass. Yet God's Word was established, and He spoke it again, establishing a covenant between them. In Genesis chapter 17, it speaks of this covenant; *1 When Abram was ninety-nine years old, the Lord appeared to Abram and said to him, "I am [a]Almighty God; walk before Me and be blameless. 2 And I will make My covenant between Me and you, and will multiply you exceedingly." 3 Then Abram fell on his face, and God talked with him, saying: 4 "As for Me, behold, My covenant is with you, and you shall be a father of [b]many nations. 5 No longer shall your name be called [c]Abram, but your name shall be [d]Abraham; for I have made you a father of [e]many nations. 6 I will make you exceedingly fruitful; and I will make nations of you, and kings shall come from you. 7 And I will establish My covenant between Me and you and your descendants after you in their generations, for an everlasting covenant, to be God to you and your descendants after you. (Genesis17:1-7 NKJV).* It was twenty-four years after God initially spoke the promise when He spoke this to Abraham. In between this time, Abraham had to believe, wait, and trust God until the manifestation. It was also pertinent for Abraham to follow God's instructions.

When God's instructions are not fully followed, it initiates a process. What is a process and how does that pertain to following God's instructions? Well let's first define process. According to Merriam-Webster Dictionary, a process is defined as a series of actions or operations conducing to an end. A process always begins with an end goal or product. It first begins with an idea and the creator of such. The creator engineers the idea, and the manufacturer produces the product. The manufacturer of a product is always given instructions in how to produce the product through systematic steps and the end goal is to have a product for a purpose and for use. God, The Creator has always had a plan and purpose for all His creation. From the beginning He already had a process in place. God is omniscient (all knowing), He knew that man was going to mishandle His original design, therefore, He had a redemptive plan, to restore mankind's original design. Even in that redemptive plan, the process included instructions. As we continue to examine what God told Abraham and Sarah and when you study the story, you will see how the covenant He stablished with them and the instructions He gave was all a part of a bigger plan and purpose. In their story, we can see a process. In this process God gave instructions, however, Sarah took it upon herself to try to make the promise of God come to pass through her handmaiden, which resulted in Abraham bringing forth Ishmael. But Ishmael was not the promised one, Isaac was. Had Sarah truly believed, she would not have taken matters into her own hands, and she would have fully followed the instructions. However, because she did not, God still provided a way to get them to the goal – which was bringing forth that promised one – Isaac. It was necessary for Isaac to be born because he was part of the seed line to Jesus, our redemptive solution. How often has God spoken to you concerning you or a matter, and you had to wait years for the manifestation? How many times have you stood on God's Word, believing that it is true and waited for it to come to pass? How many times has God given you instructions and you did not obey them? Have you ever thought that disobedience could be the reason for delay to the manifested promise? Think about it. This is food for thought.

I can think of countless times that God has spoken to me concerning a matter. Although I believed that His Words were true, it was sometimes hard to wait. I could have been like Sarah and try to take matters into my own hands. However, the wait is necessary. I found myself, many times having to hold on to hope while I waited for the manifestation. Hope is a feeling of trust; it gives us the feeling of expectation and desire for certain things to happen. Hope is attached to faith and is the very necessary component needed to walk by faith. I imagine that this is what Abraham and Sarah had to do as well.

Through the process of waiting, you learn to trust and to persevere. The very words you hold on to, are the words that are also tested. It is during the course of the testing that the faith of God is activated and causes us to stand on what we believe God has spoken. The faith of God activates and faith in God accompanied with obedience brings the manifestation. According to the Message Bible, (faith is) the fundamental fact of existence is that this trust in God, this faith, is the firm foundation under everything that makes life worth living. It's our handle on what we can't see. The act of faith is what distinguished our ancestors, set them above the crowd (Hebrews 11:1-2). Traditionally, we know this scripture to say, "Now faith is the substance of things hoped for, and the evidence of things not seen" (KJV). This scripture demonstrates that faith is trusting in God, no matter what, in all circumstances. This enables us as a believer to be steadfast and unmovable while standing on God's words at all times. The faith of God was activated in Abraham and Sarah while they waited. God said, "Sarah your wife shall bear you a son, and you shall call his name Isaac; I will establish My covenant with him for an everlasting covenant, and with his descendant" (Hebrews 11:19 KJV). Surely, what God promised came to pass. God even made a promise and established a covenant concerning his other son Ishmael, and it is so.

There is another account of having the faith of God that comes to mind. In the book of Luke, God sent His messenger to Mary with a word straight from him. *28 And the angel came in unto her, and said, Hail, thou that art highly favoured, the Lord is with thee: blessed art thou among women. 29 And when she saw him, she was troubled at his saying, and cast in her mind what manner of salutation this should be. 30 And the angel said unto her, Fear not, Mary: for thou hast found favour with God. 31 And, behold, thou shalt conceive in thy womb, and bring forth a son, and shalt call his name JESUS. 32 He shall be great, and shall be called the Son of the Highest: and the Lord God shall give unto him the throne of his father David: 33 And he shall reign over the house of Jacob forever; and of his kingdom there shall be no end (Luke 1:28-33 KJV).* God had a plan, and He communicated that plan to the one he had chosen. Mary was a believer and also had a relationship with God. Little did Mary know that the word given to her would actually usher in the redemptive plan of God for all mankind. God made a promise. Although Mary may not have understood the bigger picture of that promise, she still took God at His word and believed Him. She may have questioned the method of the plan, nevertheless she said, *"be it unto me according to your word" (Luke 1:38 KJV).* The very fact that she said, "nevertheless, be that be it *according to your word"* demonstrates how much she believed in and trusted God. Additionally, it shows her submission and willingness to obey Him. It really takes faith to be in a situation that you cannot see the way or the how, but still believe that it will happen and work out for the good!

Mary is a good example of a woman of faith having the faith of God. She submitted herself completely to the will of God and trusted the plan. Her faith was activated with a Word from God that included instructions. She willingly believed the Word of the Lord, trusted His plan, submitted and obeyed the instructions. The key here is that she believed, and she obeyed. Blessed is she who believed, for there will be a fulfillment of those things which were told to her from the Lord (Luke 1:45 NKJV). Mary's act of faith resulted in the greatest blessing. She brought forth the Lord of lords and the King of kings.

As you can see, faith is very necessary to have in order to fulfill the purposes and plans of God. When God gives a promise, it is covenant, and His Word will not turn unto void. However, we play a part in this too. When we have the faith of God, which is totally believing and having confidence in what He says, we follow through with obedience. Often times, the words spoken to us from the Lord or what we believe based on the Word of God is tested. It is during these times that opportunity is given to get to know God more and grow in relationship with Him. It is during this time that we come to know Him as more than the creator or God our heavenly father. Through experiences we may grow to know Him as Adonai our Lord & Master, or as Jehovah Jireh our provider, or as Jehovah Shalom our peace, or Jehovah Nissi the Lord our banner, or as Jehovah-Raah the Lord is my Shepherd. My personal testimony is knowing Him as all of these names, not only through hearing the word of God, but also through my own trials, tribulations and experiences with God. There were many times in my life in which I experienced Him as Jehovah Rapha the God that heals. It was during those times that I had to activate faith in order to press through and stand.

During my journey, my husband and I were tested with one of the greatest health scares of our lives. A few years ago, my husband was called by the hospital to schedule further testing based on a previous test result. The order was for him to see an Oncologist. We both were unsure about why this referral was made, but he scheduled. In my mind, I started to think many different thoughts. Why does he need to schedule an appointment with the Oncologist??? Isn't that a doctor that treats cancer??? Immediately a little panic set in, but I started to pray. What is really going on, was my thought. I began to ask God questions and seek His face. Transparently speaking, I was shaken up. I did not know what to expect. I started to think about all the unfulfilled prophecies spoken over him and over us together. However, I knew deep down in my soul that it was imperative to really pray, earnestly seek God's face and hear from Him. Although I wanted to know why, I needed to hear what to do and how to do it. I knew that it was necessary to not only hear from, but also do what He says. On the day of the appointment, I accompanied my husband to the doctor's office. Based on our questions, the doctor knew we really did not understand the depth of what was going on. The doctor shared that there were spots all over both lungs and that it was cancer. He was diagnosed with lymphoma. We were stunned, and literally sat there speechless. What did this really mean....and why God? The doctor wanted to do a biopsy to see if the cancer was even treatable at this point, but basically telling him to get his affairs in order. As we set there in shock, the Word of God immediately rose up in my heart – He shall live and not die and declare the works of the Lord! We needed a word…a specific, right now word concerning this situation! I was determined to seek the Lord and was not going to stop until I heard from Him. I was holding on to faith and speaking life according to His written Word. I looked up scriptures concerning life and living, and I spoke those words over him. In the midst of speaking, I was still thinking about all the words spoken to us through prophecy that had not yet come to pass. This could not possibly be the end, was my thought. Nevertheless, I continued to speak out loud, God's written Word.

As I sought the Lord, He spoke to me and gave me specific instructions. The faith of God was activated in me, and I was going to obey and do exactly what he specifically said to do and speak. My husband also sought God and was given a set of instructions. Meanwhile, he had lung surgery and we continued to trust God while waiting on the results. We carried on, believing God and followed His instructions. There were specific words God told me to speak. There were specific things he told me to do. I followed the instructions without wavering to the left or the right. I found that the more that I heard, spoke, and stood on His Word, the stronger my faith was. We were being built up in the midst of the storm. The Word says faith of a mustard seed moves mountains, and I was believing God to move this mountain! God spoke and we believed what he said. We just had to trust God through the process. After further testing and having the surgery, the doctor came in to share some news. He stated to us, "I do not know who you believe in or pray to…. but we no longer see the cancer! The spots have disappeared" He looked so stunned, because he was very sure of what he saw. I said, "We believe in the Most High God, Jesus is a HEALER!" This was truly a miracle. Yes, the Lord can and will do the impossible!! The doctor became a believer that day. The Word says, "Without faith, it is impossible to please Him, for he who comes to God must believe that He is, and that He is a rewarder of them that diligently seek Him" (Hebrews 11:6, NKJV). We sought the Lord, we stood on faith, and we trusted Him, but we knew that it was our obedience that manifested the healing. The life of a kingdom citizen should always prove faith. This is one of many testimonies of faith, and what God can and will do.

As a kingdom woman of faith and through my experiences with God, I know that He IS! Through this journey I have learned many lessons about the faith of God. The following are as such:

- The faith of God is a Kingdom system of belief.
- Faith is believing in who God is. It's trusting His what, when why and how.
- We must have confidence in his purposes, ways, and plans.
- Faith is also knowing that God will do what He says He will do.
- We must trust God. If we fully trust God, we will truly obey Him.
- Faith is a superpower and is behind the ability to endure tests.
- We must walk (live) by faith, and not by sight. Faith is action.
- Our system of belief must remain in the truth of God's word.

- Faith shows the power of the Kingdom.

As a believer, we must operate in and by faith. In order for us to obey God, we must first believe that He IS. When we do this, we can walk by faith and not by sight. It is imperative to remember that it pleases God, The Father, when we seek Him and obey Him. The beauty in seeking God is that it not only gives us opportunity to hear His voice but also build a relationship with Him. When we are in a relationship with the Father, we become more and more familiar with Him and His desires, will, and plans. It makes you want to please Him.

Ultimately, Jesus Christ is the greatest example of the faith of God. His relationship with the Father, His walk, His talk, and His extreme obedience manifested the power of the kingdom. It literally took the Faith of God to submit His will to the Heavenly Father's redemptive plan for man, sacrifice Himself, and die so that we may have life. What a great example that He not only demonstrated, but He also left the blueprint for us. May we continue to look to the author and finisher of our faith to carry out our assignments in the earth.

I will leave you with some scriptures on *faith* to study, meditate, believe, and live by. May your *faith* continue to increase:

Matthew 21:21
And Jesus answered them, "Truly, I say to you, if you have faith and do not doubt, you will not only do what has been done to the fig tree, but even if you say to this mountain, 'Be taken up and thrown into the sea,' it will happen."

Matthew 21:22
"And whatever you ask in prayer, you will receive, if you have faith."

Matthew 17:20
He said to them, "Because of your little faith. For truly, I say to you, if you have faith like a grain of mustard seed, you will say to this mountain, 'Move from here to there,' and it will move, and nothing will be impossible for you."

Romans 10:17
"So faith comes from hearing, and hearing through the word of Christ."

1 Corinthians 16:13
"Be watchful, stand firm in the faith, act like men, be strong."

1 Corinthians 2:5
"That your faith might not rest in the wisdom of men but in the power of God."

Galatians 2:20
"I have been crucified with Christ. It is no longer I who live, but Christ who lives in me. And the life I now live in the flesh I live by faith in the Son of God, who loved me and gave himself for me."

1 John 5:4
"For everyone who has been born of God overcomes the world. And this is the victory that has overcome the world—our faith."

Sabrina L. Clemons is a kingdom-minded woman of faith with a kingdom assignment. Her purpose is to be about her Father's business bringing glory to Him in everything she does, while speaking truth in love, life and healing, and the oracles in which the Father reveals and chooses her to speak. Ordained and consecrated in 2006, she has led different teams in ministry over the years to include Women's Ministry, Christian Education, Intercessory Prayer, and Children's Church. She has served as a Church Administrator, and in the role of Co-Pastor while her husband led Resurrection House International Ministries. Currently, her assignment in marketplace ministry is serving and leading as a regional director for a nonprofit organization and she is the founder of a budding ministry - Rising From the Ashes.

Sabrina L. Clemons is a graduate of Norfolk State University and continued her graduate studies at Hampton University. Additionally, she continues her ministry studies through the Freedom (Life) School of Ministry. She is a contributing author in the book 'Hear Me Roar. Sabrina is also the CEO of C-LYFE Unlimited. She is dedicated to providing services that stimulates and enhances growth, development, and solutions for mind, soul & spirit, while advancing the kingdom agenda. She feels especially called to the family mountain, women, and children, particularly those who have experienced trauma, and domestic & sexual violence. She coaches and mentor youth and young adults that have been victimized and/or experienced trauma in their lives. Being a survivor herself of such experiences, she easily identifies and empathize with all who has experience such. Her faith in God has empowered her to be resilient. She is determined to help others experience resurrection power, restoration, and freedom through what she offers in business and ministry. In addition to being an administrator, Sabrina is an educator and advocate that works within her community. She serves on several collaborative teams, taskforces and coalitions. She recently served as Vice-Chair on the Violence Against Women Alliance and on the High-Risk Domestic Violence Taskforce. She is the proud wife of Elder Anthony Clemons and the mother of two beautiful, gifted daughters – Rachel & Sarah.

Contact: thekingsagenda12@gmail.com

Facebook: @SABRINA SPEAKS LYFE

Chapter Seven- Letricia Brown

The Compassion of God

Compassion- The deep awareness of the suffering of another; coupled together with a desire to relieve it.

Compassing
Others openly
Mending
People,
And
Showing
Solace
Intentionally
Offending
None

Compassionate- The feeling or showing compassion/empathetic

Compass- To make a circle (a hedge around)

Without compassion there can be no preservation of mankind...without love there can be no compassion, mercy or grace. God has given to every person the ability to Love...For the love of God is shed abroad in our hearts by the Holy Spirit.

This equates "His" love, not our love is placed in our hearts by God Himself. In the last days, the love of many will wax cold, to be yet sensitive in a choosy world, especially when this compassion is viewed as soft, or weak is quite challenging to say the least.

How should I be? Sense this unpopular act of kindness is deemed a less desirable trait...even to a fault or flaw in you as a person. My son made a statement, "Be humble, be kind, but be a beast." One might say that this is a barbaric attitude to take on, but I beg to differ. You must stand up in and for what you know is right, those are attributes that causes you to be a cut above the rest. God has also dealt to every man/woman a measure of faith. What does faith have to do with compassion? I'm glad you asked!

Faith is seeing what is not visible to the naked eye. It is believing that what you hoped would happen already has. If that is the case, your desire to see victory in the life of someone that others may feel deserve the opposite. What they are receiving from you is nothing short of grace. Though again we hear God speak, "My grace will not always strive with man...yet my grace is sufficient for You!!"

If the grace of God is sufficient for me in all this, then why shouldn't my grace at best, be extended to others suffering from the impediments of reasoning beyond their control. There are unseen forces that impedes the human spirit and causes fear, don't and unbelief.

How does one have compassion on those who are challenged without being absorbed into the dire and druggy muck and mire themselves?

- Know whose you are and why you are (Purpose, destiny)
- Allow God's love to direct, lead and guide you as to any necessary interventions
- Be sure your own heart is clean, and your motives are right. No exploitation, no gloating, no self-serving, Be sincere
- Give God all the Glory

Jesus said, "when you do your alms" be secretive about it. This also includes forgiveness, restoration, care to name a few. There is simply no need to expose others' weaknesses, faults or shortcomings to others; however, we feel they deserve it. One must make sure they have gone through the healing process themselves.

"You shall know! The truth and the truth will make you free! The Christ in you will make you FREE!

The question is do we really know who and what freedom is?

Freedom- The power or right to act, speak or think as one wants without hindrance or restraint. To be unrestrained, the power of self-determination is attributed to the will; the quality of being independent to fate or necessity.

When we understand Christ's work on the cross, we understand "Free Will." I will go redeem man unto myself. His choice to die for mankind was not predicated on human incentives. Where He could've exposed the sinful adulteress, He chose to write her suitors names in the sand and called them to see themselves.

When given the opportunity to expose Judas, He invited Him to dinner. When He could have easily disembarked Peter from service because he divided them, He restored him and mightily used him for His glory.

Philippians 3:13-14- [13] "Brethren, I do not count myself to have apprehended; but one thing I do, forgetting those things which are behind and reaching forward to those things which are ahead, [14] I press toward the goal for the prize of the upward call of God Christ in Jesus."

Paul in his own eyes was great, because he thought he was the answer to all, this wrong thinking caused him to find himself saying, "This one thy I know forgetting those things that behind me."

Prayer

Eternal Father, God of all wise and true, thank you for your love for mankind, for the gift of life and peace. It is by your hand that we offer ourselves to you as instruments of your love, grace, compassion and love. As you lead and guide us by your Holy Spirit, let us extend this same grace to others from a pure heart. Teach us how to love like you.

Affirmation: Today...I will extend to others the "Grace that I have received myself!

A native of Pascagoula, MS, Apostle Letricia King Brown is the mother of three sons, Dante, Rollen Jr. (present with the Lord), Joshua, and three beautiful granddaughters and three handsome grandsons.

She is the visionary and founder of Kingdom Ministries Church, which was birthed September 2000 and serves as Senior Pastor in Newport News Virginia.

Apostle Letricia Brown gave her life to the Lord March 15, 1982, and God has proven the fruit of her labor. Chosen by God and called to the Five-Fold-Ministry in June 1983. Apostle has an awesome mantel of prophetic anointing, the fruit and gifts of the Spirit in operation, healing and deliverance ministry manifested. She has faithfully served in various capacities in ministry. She holds a Diploma in Executive Secretarial and Business Administration and has held a position as a schoolteacher in the Newport News, Virginia school district. Apostle attended Apostolic International Theological University, Duluth Georgia where she received a Doctorate in Theology. Dr. Brown is the President of Kingdom International Theological University in Newport News, Virginia. In the fall of 2020 the newly released Kingdom Living Magazine was published. The unveiling of Kingdom Global Alliance Network (KGAL) was launched October 2021.

Dr. Brown is also an entrepreneur, visionary and founder of Handmaidens of Excellence Ministry. Apostle is a published author of "The World of Four" Series (Children's Book) and "Apostle's Inspirational Quotes" and Kingdom Living Magazine. November 1, 2022, Apostle Brown signed a contract on her very first business venture, "La'She Boutique".

God had a greater vision with the birthing of K.I.N.G.D.O.M. International Ministries Inc, which serves as a covering and birthing of new ministries global. Kingdom Ministries Church, Newport News, VA, Ambassadors for Christ Worship Center, Petersburg, VA, Harvest Ministries, Waldorf, MD and Lifeline Outreach Deliverance Center, Philadelphia, PA.

Committed to the task that God has put before her not by letter, but by experience she has been tried by fire and has come forth as pure gold. Apostle has traveled to Senegal West Africa, Mexico and the Bahamas as a missionary helping hurting hearts suffering and those who are without Christ. Her desire is to see the body of Christ come together in unity, maturity and grow in love.

The scripture that truly portrays her life is found in Philippians 3:7-10. "All that I have attained: I count as loss; for the excellence of the knowledge of my Lord Jesus for whom, I have suffered the loss of all things; and count them rubbish, that I may gain Christ; and found in Him, not having my own righteousness, which is from the law; but that which is through faith in Christ. That I might know Him, and the power resurrection, and the fellowship of His suffering, being conformed by His death." Yet, I press on!

Chapter Eight- Mary Collins

The Nurturing of God

When my daughter Crystal asked me to write a chapter in her book it made me happy that she considered me. My excitement grew while she explained to me what she needed me to write about. My first thought was I did not think I could write what she was looking for but the more we talked I knew what to pray about. The more that I prayed the more God began to give me information to write about. It was like my own daughter had nurtured a need in me to share about my nurturing experience with others especially my own children.

As a mother of five children and seventeen grandchildren and nineteen great grandchildren I am very familiar with the need to nurture children so that they can become the best version of themselves. As women we are a great example of the nurturing nature of God. The nurturing process begins the very moment that we discover we are carrying a child. Everything about our lives shift including the things that we do, say, wear and eat as we have been introduced to our role as nurturer. Right from the beginning of our knowledge that a child is now growing inside of us our whole assignment is all about someone else; we have now stepped into the role of a nurturer.

There are many women and men throughout the bible who nurtured others, but the first to ever nurture was Eve. In fact, the Hebrew meaning of Eve means the mother of all living. You might be asking, did Eve already know how to nurture others since she was the mother of all living? What does it mean to nurture? Who should I nurture? Why is it so important to nurture others? You might even be wondering if you have to give birth to someone to nurture someone. All of these are great questions whether you ask them openly or inwardly.

Webster Dictionary's Definition:
verb
>   1.   *care for and encourage the growth or development of.*

noun
>   1.   *the process of caring for and encouraging the growth or development of someone or something.*

Nurturing does not just occur between a parent and a child as many may think. One of the most well-known nurturing relationships in the bible occurred between Naomi and **Ruth 1:16** *"And Ruth said, Intreat me not to leave thee, or to return from following after thee: for whither thou goest, I will go; and where thou lodgest, I will lodge: thy people shall be my people, and thy God my God."* I was nurtured by my mother Ruth Juanita Holmes and my grandmother Virgie Monk. I remember the many days where both of these powerful women of God would keep me close to them and taught me how to properly care for and manage my home. It was because of their love, diligence, and guidance that I was able to rear my children according to the nurturing ways of God.

As I look back there were four principles to nurturing my children that paved the way to guide my children through the stages of their growth and development to adulthood.

- Protect
- Provide
- Push
- Pray

April, Crystal, Melissa, Norman, Demetrius and I used to watch the "Animal Kingdom" every Saturday. The way that the lioness would fight to protect her cubs against any predators or other threats that came to harm them reminds me of my love for my children. As a mother part of the nurturing factor is to ensure that we are protecting our children from harm's way.

There are so many things that have happened in my life and the lives of my children that I could share with you when discussing the principle of a nurturing protector. The one memory that comes to mind in protecting my children is when I had to contact Mr. Redd from the NAACP to help us with an incident that occurred at my children's school. We were living in Barboursville West Virginia and my children were attending the Cabell County School District, which by the way was a predominately white school with the exception of my children.

My children were harassed so severely that there were days that they did not want to attend because of the threats, abuse, and the taunting from both the teachers and the students. The final straw came when my daughter Melissa informed my mother Ruth and I that a male student had come over to place a cone cup on her head as she was at her locker. This cup was used as a threat to represent the KKK. The pain inside as a parent knowing that your children are threatened will naturally cause the instinct of a protector to rise. This aspect of nurturing forced something to rise in me and to fight for justice for my children.

Providing for my children was one of my priorities so when the opportunity for me to become a Teacher's Assistant at my children's school I had a peace that I would be able to continue to provide financially for my children but to also be able to provide a sense of comfort for them to attend school and receive a quality of education that other children in our community received freely without taunting, prejudice or negativity.

Pushing my children beyond their own expectations was not always easy because there were times when their lack of confidence in themselves needed to be challenged. It's a natural part of life that people experience a lack of confidence or an insecurity at one time or another in their life. Like a baby bird in a nest the mother has to push her to take her first flight. If that bird does not flap her wings the mother will swoop down and catch her; only to prepare her for her next test flight. When that bird takes her first flight, she will become steadier and more confident.

Praying was a normal part of our lives in the home and instilling a love for God in my children was important. Not only was prayer a normal part of our lives in our home it was the one thing as a nurturer that I spent most of my time engaging in, for, with and over my children. I was an intercessor for my children who stood in the gap for them as they moved from adolescence to adulthood. I spent many days and nights praying that the decisions that they would make would honor God. As you know children grow and discover that they have the power of choices and decisions. Some decisions my children look back on and wish they made differently, but other decisions they know it was the grace of God that they had a praying mother who taught them the value of prayer and a relationship with God.

You see as a nurturer it is not always easy but the reward of seeing what and who you nurtured take flight in the right direction is all the reward you need.

Mary Collins was born and raised in a God-fearing home in Havre De Grace Maryland to loving parents Charles and Ruth Juanita Holmes. Charles and Ruth Holmes had eight children.

Mary attended nursing school right out of high school and has always had a passion for helping others.

Mary is married to Melvin Collins they currently reside in North Carolina. Mary is a mother, grandmother, and great-grandmother. She is loved dearly by her twenty-plus grandchildren and great-grandchildren. Mary is a minister of the gospel of Jesus Christ and a woman after God's own heart. She has followed the Word of God to raise her four children, April Monk, Crystal D. Harrison, Melissa Shelman, and Norman Miller. *"Train up a child in the way he should go: and when he is old, he will not depart from it." (Prov. 22:6.)*

Chapter Nine- Katyce Jones

The Patience of God

Patience, according to the Oxford Dictionary, is described as the capacity to accept, tolerate delay, trouble or suffering without getting angry or upset.

We all face moments where our patience wears thin. That can be with ourselves, others, and to be honest, even God's plan. In Galatians 5:22 it says, he will produce this kind of fruit in us: (meaning he will cause something to happen) and nine fruits are listed and one of them is patience. And now that I think about it, I don't believe that you can acquire any of the others, without *patience* first.

I can remember being young and really wanting to know who my father was. I would see families and friends with their fathers and could not understand; why couldn't that be my life? This feeling had caused me some real pain. I was angry, confused, frustrated, hurt and insecure. I felt abandoned, unwanted, suffered from low self-esteem, and thought I would never be good enough for anyone. I didn't know how to handle anything I was going through. So, as I got into my teenage years, I found myself starting to get in trouble and fighting anyone that I felt was coming up against me. I was so upset, because all I wanted was my father to be in my life and I felt like no one understood how important that was to me.

My mother was a great single parent of seven children. She has always been present in our lives. She was a hard worker and sometimes fell on hard times. I can remember a moment where we had to be separated, living with relatives so she could get on her feet, but she always came through. Now, it may not have been in the way that we thought it should be but eventually we were all together. We didn't have the latest clothes or the hottest new toy off the shelves, but we had her, each other, and the things we needed. She taught us, the greatest gifts wasn't what you had but who you had.

"For I know the plans I have for you "declares the Lord" plans to prosper you and not harm you, plans to give you hope and a future." *(Jeremiah 29:11 NIV)* In the middle of what seemed like complete chaos in my life, God had a plan. He had two people that would help aid in pulling me in, closer to him. In the bible it tells a story of Abraham and Isaac. When God told Abraham to sacrifice his only child Isaac on the altar. So, Abraham took Isaac to the altar and just as he was getting ready to make the sacrifice, he saw a ram in the bush that could be sacrificed instead of Isaac. The ram in the bush that God setup for me was, Bro Jay and Sister Crystal Harrison. I honestly did not know what would come of this relationship. Especially because myself and other teens in the neighborhood would run and hide when they would come through the neighborhood driving that loud church van. We could hear it a mile away and would scatter like roaches when the light came on. Eventually, they got a hold of me, and I went to church with them. I enjoyed myself so much. So much that I started spending a lot of time with their family and going to church with them became my norm.

As I became more involved in the church and developed a relationship with God, I could see and feel things in my life starting to change. But anytime I felt me loving the ones that seemed to love me, I would act out to try and push them away. That didn't only go for the people in my life but God as well. In (Deuteronomy 31:8 NIV) it says, *"The Lord himself goes before you and will be with you, he will never leave you nor forsake you. Do not be afraid; do not be discouraged."* Now, it took me a while to grasp this scripture, but it also let me know how patient God was willing to be with me. I couldn't believe that God would waste His time and energy on a child that was so messed up. I mean, my own father didn't want me, how could God? So, whenever I would do something wrong, I would instantly tell myself, this relationship is over. And even in my negative thought process, I would literally feel God tugging on my heart saying, come here daughter, daddy has you. It was those words that got to me every time because that is all I ever wanted to hear.

See, God knew patience was going to be the key to unlock the doors on the very thing I desired. (Ecclesiastes 3:1-11 NIV) talks about how there's a time for everything. During this time in my life God was pruning me. He had to get me to a place where I was willing to allow him to remove all the unwanted parts of me that were stunting my growth. It was time for me to be loose from confusion, frustration, and the pain of abandonment. It was time to improve my structure. *(Isaiah 43:18-19 NLT) says, "But forget all that-it is nothing compared to what I am going to do. (19) For I am about to do something new. See, I have already begun! Do you not see it? I will make a pathway through the wilderness. I will create rivers in the dry wastelands."* You see, when old things are removed from our lives, it gives God the opportunity to do something new. And in order for him to do something new, I needed to trust him. *(Proverbs 3:5-6 NLT) says, "Trust in the Lord with all your heart, do not depend on your own understanding."* Seek His will in all you do, and He will show you which path to take.

A few more years went by, I felt like I was growing in God and no longer just going to church. I was participating in youth activities, playing the drums, and singing with the children's choir. I seemed to have calmed down some and things were looking better. I remember my mother having to go to North Carolina for business, but I didn't know the exact business. I was about 16 years old at the time. I believe at some point my mother had a conversation with my godfather and he must've explained to her that it was important to take me along. It was my mother, my brother Waylon, my mother's friend Celestine Piggott, we called her "Chubby" and myself. So, we get to North Carolina for court and at that time, I still really didn't understand what was going on but the longer I sat in that courtroom and listened, the more I learned that it wasn't about me, and I definitely shouldn't have had to suffer for it. But because I did it helped me develop endurance, the endurance developed strength of character, and character strengthens our confident hope of salvation. And this hope will not lead to disappointment (Romans 5:3-5 NLT). Things got pretty heated in the courtroom and my brother went storming out. I followed behind him to check on him and to calm him down. Not long after court let out and I remember meeting my father in the hall. The meeting was about five minutes, if that. All I remember him saying is, I'm sorry we had to meet this way. He handed me a piece of paper with his number and address and that was it.

I had so many emotions after meeting my father. I was happy, nervous, still confused, a little frustrated, sad, but hopeful. I thought getting in contact with my father and finally being able to build a relationship with him was on the right track. I don't know if I fully processed what happened, but I know I wanted to make it work. So, a little time went by, and I wrote him a letter and waited for a response but never received one. I then called but would get no answer or someone would pick up the phone and hang it right up. So much for pruning! I fell right back into the place of feeling unwanted. I had no patience for the patience God was trying to instill in me. God was patient with me, and He let my emotions run its course, but He reminded me, daddy has you and I will never leave you nor forsake you.

I continued to try and contact him but found that my pursuit for God was more necessary. A few years had gone by, and I was getting married. Here it is 2002 and I decided to write my father a letter. I honestly don't remember exactly what I wrote but I know I mentioned that God place a great father figure in my life, and I call him dad. Along with asking him for some money for my wedding because that's the least he could do. After I sent that letter off I instantly regretted it. I wish I had never wasted my time or the ink. It wasn't about the money; I was hurt and angry that he chose to abandon me for a second time. My heart was broken all over again and I couldn't understand why. I thought God had me but yet here I am alone in this cycle of pain that felt like it would never end. *"O Lord, do not stay away! You are my strength: come quickly to my aid." (Psalm 22:19 NLT)*

In April of 2003, I married my wonderful husband Pedro Jones Jr. He has been one of my greatest supporters on this journey. I don't believe I would have made it this far without him. I remember going to my mom and asking her about my grandmother. My mom didn't hesitate to give me her name or share how sweet she was. She had nothing but great things to say about her and I wanted to meet her, but I will be honest enough to say, I was afraid of possible rejection. *(Isaiah 41:10 NLT) says, Don't be afraid, for I am with you. Don't be discouraged, for I am your God. I will strengthen you and help you. I will hold you with my victorious right hand."* So, I ended up finding a number and showing it to my mother. She said she would know the number if she saw it and that was it. I ended up calling the number and telling her who I was. She was overjoyed and so welcoming. We talked for a little while and she asked when I was coming to visit her. I was unsure at the time but continued to call her to talk and get to know her well. My hubby and I eventually made our way down to see her. She would talk to me about my brothers, my dad, and all her children. She would show me pictures of everyone. When she discussed my father, she would tell me "Be patient doll baby, your daddy will come around." Well, one day we were talking on the phone. My father just so happened to visit her while we were talking. I remember her saying, you want to talk to your daddy? Next thing I hear is, I don't want to talk to her. Why would you do that? By his tone, he was upset, and this was not the day for him to "come around." He left her house and my grandmother said, "Don't worry about it baby. It's not your fault! He needs to get over stuff between him and your mother." As much as I wanted to pretend it didn't bother me, I couldn't. I finally heard it from him, for myself. This was a different kind of pain and along with that pain came a different cry. Lord you said, when my mother and my father forsake me, then the Lord will take me up. (Psalm 27:10 KJV) See, not only did God take that place in my life He also placed Overseer Jay Harrison Sr. to take on the role as daddy. God's love is definitely sufficient for all our needs.

I learned so many things as I continued to trust God and be patient with myself. I learned what I was going through takes a process to get through. *(Proverbs 1:5 KJV) says, A wise man will hear and increase in learning, and a man of understanding shall attain wise counsel. (Philippians 4:6-7 NLT) Don't worry about anything: instead, pray about everything. Tell God what you need and thank him for all he has done. (7) Then you will experience God's peace, which exceeds anything we can understand. His peace will guard your hearts and minds as you live in Christ Jesus.* So, I thanked God for never leaving me despite my mess. For my mother loving us and never giving up on us and who was consistently present in our lives. I am thankful that my mother never gave me a negative perception about my father, and for my god parents and siblings taking me into their family as I was their own.

A couple more years went by, and I met my brother Gerald. He and I had grown to have a wonderful relationship. It was like we were in each other's lives all the time. We clicked instantly and the rest is history. Unfortunately, in 2017 my grandmother passed away. I remember I was sitting in the Salon with my best friend Liz getting our hair done and I had scrolled upon it on Facebook. I was in complete shock and broken hearted. I called my brother Gerald and talked with him a bit and asked him to keep me updated on her arrangements. I had so many questions running through my mind but one thing I didn't question was the love my grandmother and I had for each other. I was so unsure of what was to happen next but in (Proverbs 3:5-6 NKJV) it says, Trust in the Lord with all your heart and lean not on your own understanding. In all your ways acknowledge him, and he will direct your path.

I debated back and forth about attending my grandmother's service. I even told my brother I wasn't going to come. The thought of not attending haunted me daily. So, I called up my godfather and I shared all my feelings. I shared how I was so nervous and didn't know what to expect. I wasn't sure how my father or anyone else was going to respond to me being there and I didn't want to cause a scene. The only one I really knew and now had, was my brother Gerald. My dad (godfather) let me go through all the emotions and then said, how do you feel? I said, I feel like I have gone through too much in my life to be angry with him. I have built a relationship with God, and I have forgiven my father. He then said, what would make a difference? I said, I'm at a place whereas a child, I've done my part by trying to reach out and build a relationship with him. The ball is now in his court. So, I told my dad and made a promise to God. If my father makes the first move, then I will be open to building a relationship with him. My dad said, "Remember to honor your mother and your father and what?" I said, my days will be longer. (Exodus 20:12 KJV) See, what you all don't know, I should've been dead. I have gone through things that could've made me lose my mind, take my own life, and things that almost took my life. But God!!! (Praise Break) Little did I know, God had been working behind the scenes on my behalf all along.

There it was, twenty years later. I told my husband two nights before that I wanted to attend the service. We left the night before the service and settled into the hotel. The day had come, we entered the Funeral Home. It was packed and we found our way to the overflow room. I was able to grab a seat and listen to all the wonderful stories about my grandmother and the songs of encouragement. The time had come for us to exit, and we had to walk through the sanctuary. Many people before us were shaking hands as they passed by the family. I saw my father sitting on the first pew with his face in his hand. I walked by trying to quickly exit and heard my name. It was my brother. He gave me a hug and told my hubby and I that he would be out in a moment. He was still stuck in the pew. People started exiting the sanctuary and my brother came out and hugged me. We chatted for a moment and then my husband and I left.

As we got to the car, I asked my husband if he could run back and get my brother. I was so anxious to get out of there that I forgot to take a picture with him. My husband returned to let me know that my brother wanted me to come back but he didn't know why. I went back and my brother said, dad wants to meet you. I said, what? What did you tell him? He said, I just told him you were here, and he said he wanted to see you. I just kind of stood there in shock and felt extremely weak in the knees. To be honest the first thing that crossed my mind was, why now? Instantly God reminded me, you said if he makes the first move, then you would be willing and open. I was speechless and I think my brother and husband noticed that. They both let me know that they were going to be right there with me. The room all of a sudden seems small and I'm praying the muscles in my legs don't give out but I'm so glad God gives strength to the weak. (Isaiah 40:29)

The hardest thing about waiting is the wait! During this moment as I am waiting for my father to walk in the room. I honestly didn't know what to think or know how I was going to respond. I just knew I wanted to keep my promise to myself and God. In Ecclesiastes 5, Solomon warns us concerning keeping our promises. Verse 4 says, when you make a promise to God, don't delay in following through, for God takes no pleasures in fools. Keep all the promises you make to him. Verse 5 says, It is better to say nothing than to make a promise and not keep it. When I made this promise to God I took into consideration the years of work he did in me. Philippians 1:6 says, "Being confident of this very thing, that He who has begun a good work in you will complete it until the day of Jesus Christ." How could I not keep a promise to a God that was and still is, so patient with me? The God that welcomed me with open arms just as I was, cleansed me of my sins, renewed my mind, mended my broken heart, forgave me each time I messed up, and never left my side even though there were times when I left him. All these years God was tearing down, rebuilding, and testing both my father and me. There were plenty of opportunities for us to meet but the timing wasn't right. (James 1:3 KJV) says, knowing this, the trying of your faith worketh patience. We still had some growing to do. Now, here we are.

It is only the patience of God that can have a father just walk out of a room where his mother was just memorialized and stand in the face of his daughter after 20 years. I remember my father grabbed my hand and said, I don't know what to say but I'm so glad you're here. I'm sure there was a hug in there somewhere. I was in complete shock! I know at some point my soul left my body. It was as if I was sitting and watching a movie. Is this really happening? He held my hand, walking me around, and introducing me as his daughter. Some people were really taken by surprise. Especially my two brothers who didn't know about me. I could hear the whispers so clearly from people. "What did he say?, this is who?, He has a daughter? We were just sitting next to her" and it seemed like it continued until we left.

As we were getting ready to leave, my father asked if we were going to come to the repass. Now, I was a bit overwhelmed and wanted to get back to the hotel room to process what just happened and rest. My husband was going along with whatever I decided. My brother came over and suggested we come. We went for a while and hung out and then my father invited us to his house. We followed my brother to our father's house and chatted for a while. In that short amount of time I learned that my father and I were much alike. And although I really wanted to talk about us, I heard God say, just enjoy this moment. The bond between the two of you will come but it's going to take time. There was more work to be done but God was moving us both into a new season and it was a season worth waiting for.

See, we aren't born with patience, we have to learn patience! We have to be open to God, study and apply his word, we have to pray, and we have to suffer. This is a repeated cycle that will take time from God and ourselves. Believe it or not, there is glory in suffering. Who is better to teach us? because God is patience! I honestly never believed that my father and I could have the relationship we have today. I sometimes still have to pinch myself but what I do know is, I'm so glad where my dad and I are. I have no regrets about what it was. I believe God had this time ordained just for us because of what needed to be done in us individually.

I love my dad and how God has developed patience and love in the both of us. In these last 5 years we have built a great relationship and my prayer is that our story can be an inspiration to others. I pray for those who experience the absence of their father. I pray that you will overcome the pain of rejection from your earthly father by turning to our heavenly father.

Lord, you promised in your Word to be a father to the fatherless (Psalm 68:5 NIV) You are a comforter, helper, rescuer, and a redeemer. Give us patience, grace, and understanding as you do your healing work in our lives. In Jesus name, Amen!

Katyce Jones was born September 21, 1980, in Washington, DC and raised by her mother, in Williamsburg, VA along with her six siblings. She also has three brothers who live in NC. She is the wife of Pedro Jones Jr., the mother of Joy, and a teacher. Katyce hopes that her story will encourage those that are dealing with the pain of rejection and abandonment. While also recognizing that it is never too late to mend or build new relationships that have been broken or never existed in the past.

Chapter Ten- Brenda Abreu-Baker

The Grace of God

A free gift. Romans 3:24

If someone had told me that grace was a free gift from God, I would have said yeah, right. It is the type of thinking that holds us from seeing God's grace as it requires vulnerability on our part. A broken and shattered place and the torment in our mind that continues brings us to the pit of darkness. This darkness fills our thoughts with fear, doubt, and lies about who we are. This chapter will explore the meaning of grace from biblical stories and examples and self-exploration techniques that will aid us in seeing His precious gift of grace in the profound needs of our personal and spiritual life.

What is grace? In the article, *Grace of God: A Phenomenology Inquirity*, Thangbiakching Guite and Eric Soreng (2017) points to grace as the "unconditional love, the free, and undeserved favor of God." It is something you and I don't deserve nor have to work for. It's a gift from God. It's challenging to grab such meaning. Coming from a broken heart and distorted thinking makes us question if there is a God for those who have never heard of such a deity's grace. Those of us in the church are also left with questioning the grace of God over our lives. One thing that life has taught me in a place where I did not know such a deity and, as a believer, broken in the church is that God's grace is free. Neither did I deserve it when I was lost to the world and know that I am a believer in Christ Jesus. Grace is free, a gift, and calls upon all creation.

Grace in Creation

The biblical stories reveal this radiance of the grace of God in the book of Genesis, chapters two and three. The story began with God's creation, Adam, created in the image of God. After God created the man, Adam, He created the woman, Eve, out of Adam's rib.

> Then the Lord God made the man fall into a deep sleep, and while he was sleeping, he took out one of the man's ribs and closed up the flesh. He formed a woman out of the rib and brought her to him. Genesis 2:21-22

As we follow creation, Adam and Eve, we find them in chapter three. Both are naked, afraid, and hiding behind a tree after disobeying God and eating from the tree of life. Many times, we, God's creation, hide from Him. No different than Adam and Eve. The tragic consequences of the fall (sin of this world) have picked us up like a glass. And with tremendous force has thrown us against the floor of darkness. Our hearts have shattered into pieces. We look at the pieces in the darkness as our thoughts, hunted with fear and doubts of the lies that continue to keep us hiding from God's grace.

Grace in Brokenness

Our brokenness makes it difficult for us to witness the tender hands of God's grace in different areas of our life. I recalled a period in life- my adolescence and labeled by this world broken, a teenage mother—a high school graduate with a one-year-old child. The high school I attended did not bother to talk to me about college. Why? A college degree seemed far from reaching for a teenage mother like me. With the lies and pictures of impossibility painted and labels stamped on me for being a mother at a young age, they gazed at me as a broken glass, damaged in their sight. A shattered picture in the darkness that oppressed, devalued, and marginalized Black, Indigenous, and people of color (BIPOC) women historically left us searching for the pieces to put back together.

I believe that grace raises amid our afflictions, abandonment, confusion, and tears. I remembered calling one of my high school teachers and asking her for guidance in taking up a trade. In the book of Jeremiah, God says,

> I alone know the plans I have for you, plans to bring you prosperity and not disaster, plans to bring about the future you hope for. Jeremiah 29:11

It does not matter where you are in your life today; God's grace is shining on your path. Guite & Soreng (2017) states,

> Grace as a divine inspiration has been shown to indicate the experience of a spiritual assistance form the Divine that furthers one's emotional and psychological developmental process, enhancing self-efficacy, as well as change of one's world-view to a relatively positive one, all culminating to a transformed self (p. 143).

Grace is a gift from God. The gift that inspired the willingness in me to call and ask for help and guidance. It wasn't a college degree, but it was an education to further my skills. After a couple of years of working in the human service field, grace shows up. A ten-year journey, but I earned my bachelor's degree. And looking back through the lens of grace, I can attest to you that God has guided me in fulfilling my dream. This journey didn't start with me having faith; it began with the grace of God declaring that He alone knows the plan.

Grace called Jesus

God's grace promises He alone knows His plans for you and me, not the world, but God. He created us, but He did not stop there! God did something tremendous and sent his Son, Jesus, full of grace and truth (John 1:14). In chapter fourth of the book of John, we find

Jesus speaking to a Samaritan woman at a well. To her surprise, Jesus, a Jew, asked her for a cup of water. See, Jews didn't associate with Samaritans.

> The woman answered, "You are a Jew, and I am a Samaritan—so how can you ask me for a drink?" Jesus answered, "If you only knew what God gives and who it is that is asking you for a drink, you would ask him, and he would give you life-giving water." John 4:9-10

The scripture doesn't tell us her name but her ethnicity and status in society. Any one of us can identify with her if we continue reading her story; it's evidence that she was broken and with shattered dreams. Jesus continues with the conversation and tells her about living waters,

> "Those who drink this water will get thirsty again, but those who drink the water that I will give them will never be thirsty again. The water that I will give them will become in them a spring which will provide them with life-giving water and give them eternal life." "Sir," the woman said, "give me that water! Then I will never be thirsty again, nor will I have to come here to draw water." John 4:13-15

Grace showed up in a way that offered her living waters. Jesus knew that she was married five times, and the man she lived with was not her husband (John 4:16-18). Grace is a gift, and we should take it when it comes. The plan of God, redemption, came through the gift of grace, Jesus. The apostle Paul tells us in Romans chapter three,

> But by the free gift of God's grace all are put right with him through Christ Jesus, who sets them free. Romans 3:24

In the book *The Knowledge of the Holy*, A.W. Tozer (1961) acknowledges that,

Grace is the good pleasure of God that inclines Him to bestow benefits upon the undeserving. It is a self-existent principle inherent in the divine nature and appears to us as a self-caused propensity to pity the wretched, spare the guilty, welcome the outcast, and bring into favor those who were before under just disapprobation. Its use to us sinful men is to save us and to make us sit together in heavenly places to demonstrate to the ages the exceeding riches of God's kindness to us in Christ Jesus (p. 93).

Through the death of Jesus and His resurrection are how we obtain such undeserved favor from God. When grace came in the form of Jesus and told the Samaritan woman that she would never be thirsty again, she immediately replied, "give me that water" (John 4:15). Darkness fled at her response; the broken glass was made whole again. Light tore down distorted views, ripped the labels off, and dressed her in righteousness. Her heart opened to receive the free gift of grace. She was face-to-face with grace, Jesus, the Messiah who came to her and you and me. Jesus had not changed. He will always come to give you the gift of grace.

The Samaritan woman, filled with gratitude, leaves her water jars behind and begins her role as an evangelist, telling everyone in her town about the grace of God, Jesus. Once looked down in society became the one who brought grace and truth to those in darkness and oppressed. A woman with no name became grace! I, too, responded to such a great gift, and at some point, we all have to make that choice.

Guided Self-Exploration of the Grace of God

The underserved favor; grace is constantly showering us with gifts. And the darkness of our thoughts, hunted with fear, doubts, and lies, hinders us from seeing grace, Jesus. One way that I continue to uncover the grace of God in my most profound needs is through self-exploration. Self-exploration will help you see grace in your most profound personal and spiritual life needs. It helps us navigate life stages and teach us to address our brokenness and shattered lives in our childhood, adolescence, and adulthood, which can help us heal and bring closure through the scriptures. And with the help of Jesus, identify those areas that we genuinely desire to understand and see grace.

The first step starts with a question. It can be a question about your childhood, adolescence, and adulthood.

Trait: *Grace*
Step 1: Start with a Question   *"Where was the grace of God in _____ (you fill in the blank)?"*

The second step is a simple prayer.

Step 2: Start with Prayer   *"Jesus, please lead me to see your grace over my life. Let me see your healing grace in Jesus' Name!"*

The third step, write your story. It requires us to acknowledge negative experiences or situations. Writing our stories is also healing as our thinking has deprived us of different areas in our life: childhood, adolescence, and adulthood. These stages in our personal life have positively or negatively distorted our views of how we see "self" in the natural and the spiritual. In both the natural and spiritual life, one must find meaning and healing in those areas. It may be challenging but needed to overcome periods that have impacted our natural and spiritual senses.

Step 3: Write Your Story. Stages in your life that you may want to explore, for example: childhood, adolescence, and adulthood.

The fourth step is to review and read your story to yourself and identify areas in your personal life where you can see God's grace demonstrated, i.e., a parent, aunt/uncle, spouse, teacher, friend, or stranger.

> **Step 4: Review/Read Your Story to Yourself: Identify areas in which God's grace was demonstrated, for example, a parent, aunt/uncle, teacher, friend, stranger, etc.**

The fifth step, write and study the scripture. Studying the scriptures is the beginning of seeing and understanding how God's grace has touched different areas of your life.

> **Step 5: Write a scripture (s). Go back to step 4 and write the scriptures in the areas where you identify God's grace.**

The final step, meditate on the scripture(s) and write a prayer. Meditating on God's grace as his word leads to healing and transformation.

Step 6: Mediate on the scriptures and write a prayer of the grace of God.

These biblical stories (there is more grace in the bible) are reminders to stimulate us to wholesome thinking. It helps us construct our story and meaning through self-exploration. In pursuing to understand, learn, and identify the grace of God in the profound needs of our personal and spiritual life. God's grace means that it is an undeserved favor given to us as a gift. And no one can take it such a marvelous gift, Jesus. Our story is a vital part of the extraordinary story of redemption. His redemption is motivated in love and carried by grace for His creation. As created in the image of God, we bear His grace through Jesus!

Brenda Abreu-Baker has served in the ministry for 17 years alongside her husband, Dr. Parris Baker, as co-Pastor, at Believers International Worship Center, Inc. Brenda received her Master of Social Work from Edinboro University. She is passionate about working in the human service field with diverse populations. Her research interest includes evidence-based practice, spirituality, psychological well-being, and improving direct interventions that empower poor and underrepresented Black, Indigenous, and people of color (BIPOC) and marginalized communities. She oversees Beauty for Ashes Women's Ministry and Mother Baker's Prayer Line- an outreach designed to mobilize women from all walks of life, where she continues to promote the mission of restoration of families built solidly on the truth of the Word of God and the finished work of Christ Jesus. Brenda is the mother of three children Bremont, Samantha, and Jonathan.

Chapter Eleven- Crystal D. Harrison

The Purpose of God

Our purpose is always for someone else.

I hope that by reading this chapter you will discover that we have each been created with a purpose for a purpose by the One who gives purpose. Now is your time to walk in that purpose. The Father already had a plan for your life my friend. Let's take this journey together so that you can understand why you must get focused and walk in the purpose of God for your life. **Romans 8:28 "And we know that for those who love God all things work together for good, for those who are called according to his purpose."**

The scripture Jeremiah Chapter 1:5 has special meaning for me, which details purpose waiting on our arrival into the world. It was through my daughter Juanita's pregnancy with Jeremiah that God showed me that no matter what path we choose to take when we are obedient and surrender our will to Him, He will forgive us and turn what we consider to be a mistake into a blessing.

I failed initially in seeing God's hand in what was occurring in her life. I was looking through the wrong lenses at the time of my discovery. So many of us fail the test of waiting because we focus on the obstacles that seem to be present and not the purpose that is waiting. I have an enormous amount of love, respect and honor for Juanita Nicole Woodson because you my dear, have taught me how to see the purpose in some of the most challenging times of our lives. Her pregnancy had purpose! She has purpose! Jeremiah Lavan Harrison has purpose! And now everyone connected to her is discovering their purpose because she allowed God to use her purpose!

Women of God you have purpose! No matter what your situation may be, regardless of your delays, no matter the mistakes you have made in this life understand that God created you with a purpose, for a purpose to be used as a purpose in the life of someone else. It is not too late to discover and walk in your purpose. You may be in the prime of your life or feeling like I am old can God use me? Yes! God is not a God concerned about age He is concerned about purpose. In the words of my husband Overseer Jay T. Harrison Sr. "you are God's greatest concern." **"Isaiah 40:31 "But they that wait upon the Lord shall renew their strength; they shall mount up with wings as eagles; they shall run, and not be weary; and they shall walk, and not faint."** Get up, let's grow and get our purpose on!

Jeremiah 1:5 "Before I formed thee in the belly I knew thee; and before thou camest forth out of the womb I sanctified thee, *and* I ordained thee a prophet unto the nations."

God already knew the paths that each of us would take in our lives. The U-turns, the dead ends, the stops, yields, and even the direction challenges. The Father had a GPS plan for all of our purpose detours all along. Get up, get moving and get your purpose on. Ephesians **1:4 He hath chosen us in Him before the foundation of the world, that we should be holy and without blame before Him in love."**

What is purpose? Who gives purpose? What happens if we can't find or discover our purpose? What do we do with our purpose? Can I forfeit my purpose? I have asked myself all of these questions at one time or another in my life: perhaps maybe more than once. It is perfectly ok if you ask yourself these questions but be willing to find the answers necessary for you to learn grow, walk in and ultimately lead others in the discovery of their purpose.

When Jesus was here on earth His purpose was very clear and well defined from the Maker. In fact, even on the cross Jesus surrendered His will to the will of the Father to fulfill His purpose on earth. Jesus did not have to spend years attempting to discover His purpose, he was birthed into His purpose. As are we; God knew why He created each of us. **John 18:37 "Pilate therefore said unto him, Art thou a king then? Jesus answered, Thou sayest that I am a king. To this end was I born, and for this cause came I into the world, that I should bear witness unto the truth. Every one that is of the truth heareth my voice."**

Jesus also understood that His purpose came directly from the Father. Do you know where your purpose comes from? **John 6:38 For I came down from heaven, not to do mine own will, but the will of him that sent me.**

So, let's start here what exactly is purpose?

Merriam-Webster's Dictionary describes purpose as **a noun the reason for which something is done or created for or which something exists.** Webster's further describes the **verb of purpose as such to have as one's good intention or objective.**

You might be wondering where does my purpose come from? Our purpose comes from God. In **Jeremiah 29:11** God was reminding Jeremiah that, I got this just be still.

"For I know the thoughts that I think toward you, saith the Lord, thoughts of peace, and not of evil, to give you an expected end." It is in this passage of scripture Jesus actually raised his voice at Jeremiah because Jeremiah was becoming frustrated and whiney because the people around him were complaining and murmuring because the prophies that he shared didn't occur right away. Further Jeremiah's life was in danger so that also increased his worries about his current situation and why things did not seem to be happening for him as he anticipated.

I don't know about you but there have been times in my life where God showed me something, but it did not come to pass in the time I expected. Let me say this God does not need our help He simply needs our faith to trust Him.

Regardless of life's experiences God has an expected end of greatness for your life, my life, and the lives of everyone that He has created. So many times, when the challenges of life occur, we believe that God will have no use for us, but in all actuality, God wants to use us even during the storms of life. All things will work for your good when we obey Him. You might very well be reading this chapter and saying to yourself that God cannot use you because of your past. God sent me to remind you that your past is in the sea of forgetfulness.

Micah 7:19 "He will turn again; he will have compassion upon us; he will subdue our iniquities; and thou wilt cast all their sins into the depths of the sea."

So, you see my friend that abortion that you had at your weakest moment, failed marriages, bad financial stewardship, forgiven. All of your mistakes forgiven so let's get focused and get your purpose on.

Like most women we often find ourselves struggling with the answer to the question about what our purpose is. What our purpose is, is an age-old question that every human being has been faced with at some point in their life.

As a lifelong educator I remember asking my students "what do you want to be when you grow up?" What I should have been asking or equipping my students with at a young age is "how are you going to become who God created you to be when you grow up?"

Purpose is not our choice it is our discovery. Our identity crisis is because we have been taught to go find our purpose and not to discover our purpose. Understand this before the foundation of the earth your purpose was already established for you. More than likely, you were operating in your purpose all along and saw it as a nine to five job, a hobby or just something to pass the time along and not your gifted purpose from God. I believe just like Jesus we have all been created with a divine purpose for our lives. As I initially stated we are responsible for trusting God to reveal His purpose in our lives. Sometimes we all need a helping hand in discovering our purpose from someone God has assigned to cultivate and guide us along that discovery path to our purpose. I am grateful for those folks who have guided me and continue to guide me.

There was a season in my life when I was unsure of what my purpose was or the direction that I should go in to find it, but there was something inside me that I knew my purpose was greater than me or what I wanted to do. What I did know was that whatever God wanted me to do would impact lives for the better. However, there was that feeling of being lost because as I looked at everyone else around me, they seemed to know what their purpose was. Sure, there were ideas that I believed could be in my future that would lead to a divine purpose for me. But what were they? How could I tap into them? Would they be unveiled in my old age, or would I be young enough to enjoy my purpose? It was not until I married, had children, and moved to Virginia that my purpose began to be revealed to me where I understood it. Ironically enough I was already operating in my gift very early on through my babysitting for children in my teenage years. Well, who would have known? So many times, we are already doing what we were created to do.

We are taught early that college is where we will find out what we should do or become. College is not the "Purpose Locater" this is very misleading. It is important that you understand that when we enter this world our purpose has already been carved out for us by God. I am not against higher education; I am against folks stating that if you do not attend college you will be unable to discover your purpose for life. I believe that while in college your purpose may be revealed to you, but it is not created there. I didn't find my purpose at Hampton University. I did not find my gift at the University of Phoenix; what I did do at both of these places of learning was glean information about sharpening and implementing my purpose for the Kingdom of Heaven.

There have been many women in my life who have played intricate roles that would ultimately push me to the forefront of my purpose. My mother Mary Elizabeth Collins, my grandmother Ruth Juanita Holmes, Helen Bowman, the late Roxanne Surles, my spiritual mother Bishop Kim A. Davis, Elder Carla J. Smith and while not a female my spiritual father Bishop Stanley K. Smith. There will be individuals that God assigns to you who that regardless of the mess, messiness and mistakes of your life will never delete, mislead, or betray your trust and friendship; these folks right here are those people for me. In spite of all the challenges of life that I have gone through some of which were self-inflicted I am continuing to discover other dimensions to my purpose because I did not refuse to listen to the voice of those assigned to me in various stages or seasons of my life. God will assign who and what we need to help us discover our purpose. You must be willing to listen to the voice of your mentor, follow the instructions of your mentor, sow into your mentor and grow with your mentor.

Having met the late Roxanne Surles further changed my life forever. Sister Surles as we affectionately knew her was quirky, funny, and old fashioned but she had standards and a desire to guide others into their purpose. Honestly it was not until later in my life that I realized what Roxanne Surles was to me; she was a mentor, she poured into me so selflessly and I honored the gifts that she had to love others unconditionally. God will allow folks to be placed right in your path so they can open doors to the purpose that God created for you before you ever arrived on the scene. Sister Surles loved children, but she often confided that teaching children was not her passion. "Sister Crystal this is you, your heart lights up when you teach." As I began to seek God more about my purpose He began to reveal "you were born for this."

Your purpose is never for you as I quickly began to learn. The move to Williamsburg, Virginia was the catapult that would eventually reveal to me what my purpose was and how it would be used. Somewhere along the line after moving to Lafayette Square Apartments in Williamsburg I became the neighborhood "daycare lady." Families that I never met prior to them knocking on our door began to request me to care for their children. For many people this was just Sister Crystal watching children while families worked or ran errands, but to me it was an assignment. An assignment that I took very seriously to the point that I began to change the look of our home into a school. I remember that when my now best friend Helen Bowman came for an initial Head Start Home Visit for our children, she was amazed that everywhere she looked it resembled a school setting. More specifically, it was God finally answering my prayer about my purpose.

Being able to sow into other individuals who are in search of their purpose in the ECE (Early Childhood Education) Profession is now my purpose turned into passion. Our purpose in never for us to hold or covet to ourselves.

Regardless of where you are, what path your purpose takes you on your purpose should never be used as a tool to hold others back or prevent someone from growing in their purpose. There have been multiple times that I was growing and learning in the Early

Childhood Education profession, and I sought help from folks who I did not know saw me as competition or a threat and not a teammate refused to help me discover resources for growth. I made up my mind that helping other ECE professionals discover their purpose would be my mission.

One of the most disappointing missed opportunities at being able to help someone discover their purpose was recently when I hired a PCA who was assigned to a student at my center. There was something there, something about the way she interacted with the students. After speaking with her I discovered that she was making far less than what we would pay her. She decided to accept the job for a better opportunity, to provide an opportunity for her daughter and to pursue her purpose in education. However, she did not join our team because someone failed to see the value in her pursuing her purpose simply wanted to keep her potential gifts for themself. The discovery of your purpose will have haters! There will be people even those close to you who will attempt to block you, hinder you or even spiritually kill you. **John 10:10 The thief cometh not, but for to steal, and to kill, and to destroy: I am come that they might have life, and that they might have it more abundantly.**

Be willing to stand out and be different. I remember a conversation with my grandmother telling me "Crys, there is something different about you, don't be afraid of it." Honestly for a long time I was petrified of being different, not blending in; from the way I liked to dress to the way that I carried myself. I have come to terms with the fact that I am different, that I love wearing long skirts, that I speak differently and that seeing other people fulfill their purpose gets me excited.

Prayer for Purpose

Father, I pray that the reader of this chapter will seek You in the discovery of their purpose and Your desire for how to impact the world with the purpose that You have gifted to them. Father assign someone to each of them individually who will share the anointing on their life with them as my spiritual mother Bishop Kim A. Davis has shared with me to cause growth to occur in areas of my life that I never would have imagined possible. Give them endurance and a willingness to submit to the voice of the mentor that You have placed in their lives. Allow Your strength to be their strength in this discovery of purpose so that when disappointments, failures and delays arise they will find comfort in knowing that the Lord will never leave them nor forsake them.

1 Chronicles 28:20 "And David said to Solomon his son, Be strong and of good courage, and do it: fear not, nor be dismayed: for the Lord God, even my God, will be with thee; he will not fail thee, nor forsake thee, until thou hast finished all the work for the service of the house of the Lord."

Father, I pray that doors of opportunities be made readily available to them to aid them in the discovery of their purpose from You. I further pray that as this discovery is being revealed to them that they remain humble, compassionate, and hungry to discover every aspect of Your expectations for their life. Teach them Father the importance of sowing into others Father and how their selfless act of sharing You with others will open the door to purpose for so many others.

In Your Mighty Name
Amen

Crystal Denise Harrison is truly a woman after God's own heart. She strives to "Raise the Standards" one opportunity, one woman and one purpose at a time. She currently resides in Chester, Pennsylvania with her husband and family. She has been married to a phenomenal man of God for thirty-seven years, Overseer Jay Timothy Harrison Sr. the Pastor of True Vine Missionary Full Gospel Baptist Church. Jay is also the former Overseer for the Eastern District in the State of Pennsylvania under the leadership of the Full Gospel Baptist Church Fellowship International. Crystal is a wife, mother, grand-mother, community leader, mentor, friend, lifelong educator, and Pastor. Crystal and Overseer Harrison have eight children: four sons, four daughters, and seven grandchildren, with one on the way.

Crystal accepted Jesus Christ into her life at a very early age; but rededicated her life to Jesus Christ in 1991. She was ordained as a minister in Williamsburg, Virginia by the Late Edward G. Clemons. She was later ordained as an Elder in 2005 in Chester, Pennsylvania by Overseer Jay Timothy Harrison Sr. Crystal is the founder of CDH

Ministries and Heart 2 Heart. Heart 2 Heart provides an opportunity to restore the hearts of women one opportunity at a time through mentoring, fellowship and teaching, so that women can truly experience God's purpose moving in their lives as He created and intended for them to live. Crystal believes that her desire to allow God to use her compassion and purpose in the lives of others will be a guide to many along their journey.

Crystal is a graduate of Hampton University where she earned her bachelor's degree education. Crystal continued on to earn her master's degree in Early Childhood Education from the University of Phoenix.

Crystal wrote her first book "How to Fight Fair in Marriage" in 2018 after her marriage was tested and tried. As other tests in her life she fought and won in "the ring of marriage." Her book may be purchased on Amazon.

Contact: 4cdhministries@gmail.com

Website: www.CDHMinistries.com

Facebook: Crystal Harrison / Heart 2 Heart

This is a blank copy of the Guided Self-Exploration created by Brenda Abreu-Baker to help you as you study the 11 Traits of a Woman of God.

Guided Self-Exploration of the: _____

The first step starts with a question. It can be a question about your childhood, adolescence, and adulthood.

Trait: _____

Step 1: Start with a Question.

Step 2: Start with Prayer.

Step 3: Write Your Story. Stages in your life that you may want to explore, for example: childhood, adolescence, and adulthood.

Step 4: Review/Read Your Story to Yourself: Identify areas in which God's _____ was demonstrated, for example, a parent, aunt/uncle, teacher, friend, stranger, etc.

Step 5: Write a scripture (s). Go back to step 4 and write the scriptures in the areas where you identify God's _____

Step 6: Mediate on the scriptures and write a prayer of the grace of God.

References

Bible Study Tools (2022). *Mathew Henry Commentary.*

Mark 12 Commentary - *Matthew Henry Commentary on the Whole Bible (Complete)* (biblestudytools.com)

Merriam-Webster Dictionary

Wuest, Kenneth S. (1988). *Wuest's Word Studies: From the Greek New Testament.*

Wm B. Eerdmans Publishing Company, Grand Rapids, MI

Guite, T. & Soreng, E. (2017). Grace of God: A Phenomenological Inquiry. *International Journal of Indian Psychology, Vol. 4*, (4).

Tozer, A.W. (1961). *The Knowledge of the Holy.* New York, NY: HarperCollins.

www.Grace4Purposeco.com

Made in the USA
Middletown, DE
06 May 2023

29593385R00071